A Graduate's Guide to
Financial Decision Making

by

Shawn Finn, CFP®

ISBN-13: 9781546583073
ISBN-10: 1546583076
Library of Congress Control Number: 2017907483

Table of Contents

Chapter 1

Well, Hello Graduate

Congrats on your graduation.

Let's try that again because I'm not sure I've captured the intended enthusiasm. CONGRATULATIONS ON YOUR GRADUATION!!

It's truly a big deal and an achievement you should be very proud of. This is twelve years in the making. To put this in perspective, you were five or six years old when you started this journey. You probably thought this day would never come, but it has, and now you're staring at the rest of your life. Some of you may be saying, "Holy crap, now what?" and others may be saying, "Bring it on!" Whichever camp you fall into, you'll be faced with financial decisions that have been made on your behalf up until now.

This book is meant to give you the guidance you'll need to begin making the correct financial decisions immediately upon shedding that ceremonial cap and gown.

But first, before you go off to celebrate and potentially do something that you'll regret, read these pieces of wisdom; they may just save your financial life. Oh, and I've added a couple of employer peeves as well.

General Dos and Don'ts

Here are some tips for your graduation night (I had better not catch you rolling your eyes as you read these):

- Don't drink and drive on your graduation night or ever for that matter. If you've had too much to drink, call your parents, a taxi, Uber, or an Amish buggy (if in rural Indiana), or walk home. Just don't drink and drive. DUI (driving under the influence) tickets suck, are costly, and don't sound very good in an interview. Plus, you don't want to hurt anyone and have that on your conscience or have your wages garnished for the rest of your life.

- Don't get a face tattoo or anything below the wrist or above the neckline. Do you think Mike Tyson looks employable with that stupid thing on his face? I realize that isn't his only issue.

- Don't make a baby on graduation night or until you're financially ready. I'm not telling you to wait until age forty-five like me, but don't do it at seventeen, eighteen, or nineteen. Nothing will change your financial outlook quicker than a baby at your age.

- If you're one of those kids who wear their pants down to their knees, pull your damn pants up! No one wants to know what underwear you're wearing and frankly, WTF? Plus, your employment prospects are pretty limited with that ridiculous look. Sorry if I've offended anyone, but that's reality.

- Think twice or even three times prior to posting pictures or comments that may be deemed distasteful on Facebook, Snapchat, Twitter, etc. Employers have a tendency to look through social media when considering applicants and even after you've been hired. Don't friend anyone from your workplace on Facebook that may be friends with the boss. Drunken or late-night rants seem to find a way back to the wrong individuals, especially if they go viral. Getting hammered and doing stupid crap is pretty funny in the moment but not so much, come Monday morning around the office cooler.

That may have seemed like a lecture but it wasn't the intent. I simply want you to be calculated in your decisions from this point forward and side step any additional stress, that a momentary lapse in judgement may bring. Now that that's out of the way, how about your finances?

Each and every one of you will have come from a different background (unless you're twins) and will have varying degrees of experience with money management. Some of you may have read books on the subject, researched various topics on the Internet, or perhaps even completed course work on the topic during your high school career. In general, however, high school curriculums have failed to prepare students for their financial future. Money Management 101 was always intended to be learned in the home, similar to sex education, and we all know how the latter turned out. This book is meant to help you establish a financial foundation to ensure that you get off to the best possible start and are protected against unforeseen dangers that can disrupt your financial future. This is intended to supplement the education you've received over the past four years (for most of you), and no matter whether you are heading off to college in the fall or breaking into the workforce next week, there is important information in this book for everyone.

I purposely left this material short because I didn't want to overwhelm you with too much information, especially after cramming for finals over the past couple of weeks. This is the condensed version of a thousand other books on financial planning but gets into specific and relevant examples that you'll soon face and purposely walks you through important upcoming decisions/ processes step by step.

It's getting boring already, isn't it? My apologies.

How about we take a break for a pop quiz (two questions) just to make sure we're all in the right frame of mind? You should be able to do this first one in your head, so don't worry about grabbing a calculator (phone) or a pen and scratch paper.

A train leaves a depot in Chicago heading for Seattle at one o'clock central standard time traveling at fifty-six miles per hour. A similar train is leaving Salt Lake City bound for Milwaukee at noon mountain time, traveling at seventy-eight kilometers per hour with a stiff tailwind. At what time will these trains intersect, and what time zone will the trains be in when they intersect? The answer is…who cares? You're done with these stupid questions. Let's focus on the day-to-day survival tips you'll need to make it on this big scary journey you're about to embark on.

Second question (this is a fun one):

If I asked you whether you would rather receive $1 million right now, or receive a penny today and double that investment every day for thirty days, which would you choose? That's a no-brainer, right? Take the million and call it a day. If you do the math, you'll find that you would be missing out on approximately $4.36 million by taking the $1 million up front. I thought about posting a chart to illustrate the numbers, but it's pretty easy to do. Pull out your phone calculator, start with 0.01, and multiply it by 2 to double it. Repeat this calculation thirty times and you'll end up with roughly $5.36 million. Of course, either option is a lot of money, but the second option illustrates the power of compounding savings over time, and at your age, that's one thing you have a lot of: TIME. This book isn't necessarily about making you rich, but if that were an ancillary result, I'd be fine with that, and I'm sure you wouldn't hate me for it. What this book is about is making the right decisions to put you in the best possible position, no matter what your future holds.

Now, full disclosure, I struggled with how I was going to present this information to graduates. Would I be able to relate to individuals nearly three decades younger than I am? Would you even care enough to read these pages, and is the information really that important?

Doing some research online, I came across a survey from 2011 conducted by the investment firm Charles Schwab. The survey stated that 86 percent of sixteen- to eighteen-year-olds surveyed said they would rather learn about money management in a class rather than make bad decisions in real life. The year 2011 was a while ago, I admit, but through discussions with my nephew, a college freshman at the University of Texas, and several others here in Minneapolis, Minnesota, I learned not much has changed. My nephew's high school in Houston still hasn't adopted a personal money-management curriculum, nor have any in my residential state of Minnesota, or nearly any other state in the United States for that matter. There's a need, and young adults do care.

I've laid out the material from the most important to the "nice to know" so that if I do lose your attention, at least you've covered the life-changing concepts first. I've also included a checklist at the very end that captures everything you need to remember. I'm confident, however, that you'll read this book from cover to cover and hopefully refer to it from time to time as you tackle every new financial challenge.

Why I Care

I wouldn't want to take direction from someone unless I knew a little about his/her background and motive. So here it is. I hope you're thoroughly impressed (that's sarcasm, by the way).

I graduated high school back in 1988. Eighty-eight, eighty-eight, eighty-eighty-eighty-eighty-eight! Pep rally humor, anyone? Anyone? Sorry. As I was saying, I graduated in 1988 from Milton High School in rural southern Wisconsin. I wasn't what you would call a Rhodes Scholar, but I wasn't an idiot either (although originally, I spelled it "roads scholar"). I liked to think of myself as an underachiever—unmotivated, you might say. I'm assuming a few of you out there may be able to relate. I kicked around the idea of going to college but ultimately decided to enter the workforce as soon as I graduated high school. I went to work for a wilderness lodge and canoe outfitters on the Gunflint Trail near the city of Grand Marais in northern Minnesota. The pay wasn't great, but we had a blast fishing and drinking, and I had the privilege of meeting some awesome people along the way. This was a seasonal job, and once it was over, I moved back in with my parents in Milton and worked at a motorcycle and ATV parts warehouse for the next eight months. Nothing like a manual-labor job to get you to reflect on your life and question your long-term prospects. It wasn't as bad as detasseling corn but not something I could envision doing the rest of my life. Those of you in corn country will understand that reference, the rest of you should Google detasseling and thank your parents for not subjecting you to this gulag-type torture.

I realized that I didn't have it all figured out or, in all actuality, the slightest idea what I was going to do with my life, and it seemed that all my friends did indeed have everything figured out. I decided to enroll at a community college the following year back in Ely, Minnesota, on the outskirts of the Boundary Waters Canoe Area. For those of you not familiar with the greater Ely area, that's nearly as far north in Minnesota as you can go without becoming a Canadian citizen. While in Ely, I obtained an associate's degree in applied science. Those were two of the best years of my life, living in one of the most beautiful places in the United States. But alas, I still didn't know what I wanted to do.

One day, while sitting in the guidance counselor's office, I spotted a brochure of a student sitting on top of a mountain looking down on a college campus. This was Montana State University in Bozeman. You may be seeing a trend develop. I wasn't necessarily following a course of study as much as I was searching for the next beautiful place to live and, secondarily, attend school. I knew I wanted to help the environment, perhaps as an environmental engineer. But I found out that that course of study required too much math and physics, so the next best option was geology / environmental science. Two semesters of calculus, three semesters of physics, and a hell of a lot of geology courses later, I had a bachelor of science degree in geology.

My postcollegiate travels took me to Anchorage, Alaska, back to Wisconsin, on to Bryan, Ohio, back to Bozeman, back to Wisconsin, and ultimately to Minneapolis, Minnesota. I finally settled in Minneapolis where I met my wife and as I turned forty-five, we welcomed our baby girl.

I glossed over a large segment of time just to spare you several minutes of your life that you'll never get back. What I want you to glean from that background narrative is that life has many different roads that lead to your ultimate destination, whatever that turns out to be. If you haven't figured it out yet, don't stress out; you will. The path I took provided me an opportunity to do some interesting work and meet some great people, and I owe a very large part of that journey to my parents, who supported my whims not by handing me money but by encouraging me to figure it out along the way.

I'm not advocating for a college education, but you may find that getting a job right out of high school isn't what you thought it would be. You may come to the realization that you want a new direction. My degree provided me an opportunity to do some interesting work in geology and environmental remediation (cleanup) around the United States. The problem was that environmental remediation doesn't happen in places that one would typically choose to live (Gary Indiana, the Cicero neighborhood of Chicago, etc.) and the travel aspect was a killer after a while. I was on the road for nearly eight months out of the year.

As I stated above, I finally settled down in Minneapolis and started my second career in finance. There isn't a lot of correlation between geology and finance, but that didn't matter. The firm I was associated with was looking for motivated individuals who could pass a series of exams, become certified to sell securities (stocks, bonds, etc.), and learn financial planning through years of training and client interactions. At the time of this writing, I've been with the same financial institution for fourteen years, obtained my Series 7, 66, and insurance licenses, and ultimately received the Certified Financial Planner and Chartered Retirement Planning Counselor designations. More importantly, I've created and reviewed thousands of financial plans and know the problems facing individuals from high school to retirement and what it takes to make the right financial decisions to ensure you get off to a good start and stay on track throughout your lifetime (the preceding is the portion that was meant to impress you).

I would be remiss if I didn't point out that when I was your age, I made many of the same mistakes that I'll be guiding you through. Books like this didn't exist back then, and even if they had existed, I'm not sure my school district would have cared enough to provide me with the knowledge to make informed decisions around my finances or life in general. Otherwise, I could have been a millionaire by now. Damn Milton School District!

On a more serious note, I do have another reason for getting this book into your hands. A few years ago, a family member came to me and asked about declaring bankruptcy. He had traveled a less-than-successful path after high school. He went directly into the workforce and puttered around with odd jobs. He tried college for a semester and determined it wasn't for him. He went back into the workforce. One Friday night, while blowing off steam with some buddies, he had a momentary lapse in judgment. He grabbed a rope swing, launched himself off the side of a hill, and proceeded to drop twenty feet onto his uninsured arm. No big deal, right? His parents would cover his medical bills, or, worst-case scenario, the state would cover the expenses, right? No and no. He wasn't covered by his parents' health insurance, because he wasn't enrolled in college, and his parents didn't have the $45,000 to pay his debts. The state allowed him to be treated but wouldn't pay the bill. He was staring at $45,000 in medical bills and a collection agency calling him day and night to honor his obligation. He wanted to get his life back on track and thought bankruptcy was his ticket to starting over. All this could have been avoided had he known the information enclosed in these pages. I'm going to make sure you have the knowledge so this doesn't happen to you. Point of clarification: I can give you the information; only you can ensure this doesn't actually happen to you.

What Do You Want for Yourself?

Now that I've earned your unwavering respect, let's get into it, shall we?

Do me a favor, and pull out your laptop, tablet, phone, or, if you want to kick it old school, a piece of paper and pen. Take a moment, close your eyes, and just think about your goals in life. Hold on a second, I told you to think about your goals in life, not the girl or boy you've got the hots for. Come on, focus! I want you to list out, chronologically, what you would like to accomplish from today through the next ten years. But first open your eyes, or that list may be unreadable. On the left side of the page, list the goal, and be as specific as possible. On the right side, list the timeframe in which you would like to accomplish this goal. Write down everything. I'll wait.

This may seem like a waste of time, but you can't gauge progress or success if you don't define the goals you're working toward. Plus, it can be a fun exercise if you allow your imagination to run wild. Oh, and if you are writing these out (old school), leave a few spaces at the very top.

Need help getting started? What kind of job do you want? What type of salary are we talking about? Where do you want to live? Is travel important? What type of relationship are you looking for (if any)? Do you want kids? If so, by when? What kind of car do you want? (Note: That kid question may dictate the answer to the car question.)

Is that all you've got? I said write down everything.

Now take a few minutes to look at your list. Kind of overwhelming, isn't it? How the hell are you going to accomplish everything? I'll let you in on something, you won't. You may get your dream car, that aforementioned girl or boy of your dreams, the apartment on the Upper East Side of Manhattan, the $400,000 job on Wall Street or in Palo Alto, but chances are you won't accomplish everything on the list. That isn't a bad thing, and I'll tell you why. This list is going to change about a thousand times, and that's why it may be beneficial to have an electronic version to allow you to eliminate old dreams and document new and more relevant dreams along the way. On second thought, keep all the dreams in this list from today on, and when you review this document twenty years from now, you'll have a good laugh. You never know whom you'll meet along the way who will change your perspective on life. What's important at age eighteen, twenty-five, or thirty-two may not be important at forty. Trust me on this.

Next, on the same page, in the space I asked you to leave at the top, write/type these words:

- Health insurance
- Establish a cash reserve (TAKE PRIDE IN BEING DEBT-FREE)
- Disability insurance
- Start saving toward retirement

If that was first on your list already, then you're either sick or a liar, and remember, nobody likes a liar.

Chapter 2

Establishing Your Foundation

How do you do it? How do you make sure you're making all the right financial decisions so you don't end up racking up credit-card debt and medical bills, living paycheck to paycheck, or working until you're old and miserable? There isn't one plan of action that is right for every individual, owing to family support, social networks, work ethic, and at times, flat-out bad luck. There are certain components that will give you the best chance for success, however, and explaining them is the purpose of this book. If you aren't better off after reading this book, then I haven't done my job.

Establishing a foundation isn't a sexy topic, but it is a necessity. The financial foundation represents just that, a foundation, similar to that of a house. This is the slab of cement and footings that keep your financial house stable. The ingredients include health insurance, a cash reserve, ongoing cash flow / budget, and the proper level of disability insurance to protect you from a life-altering illness or injury, by insuring your most valuable asset: your ability to earn an income.

Your life will be filled with ups and downs, and it's this foundation that determines how long the down periods last and how you emerge on the other end.

Health Insurance

Historically, the debt that causes the most bankruptcy filings in the United States is medical expense debt. There were nearly two million bankruptcies in 2013 due to unpaid medical bills (CNBC, 2013). That's a shocking statistic, albeit old but not outdated. With that in mind, the first thing I'll ask you to do is talk to your parents and ask whether you are still covered by their workplace insurance plan, and if so, for how long. The adoption of the Affordable Care Act (ACA) in 2010, also known as Obamacare, was partially intended to address the issue of young adults transitioning between school and an employer that offers health care. Some of your parents' employer plans may cover you until age twenty-six, but I don't want you to take that legislation as gospel, especially with the Trump administration's repeal of the Affordable Care Act. Please ask your parents to speak with their human resources contact at work or call their plan provider to find out for sure. Get an answer, one way or another.

If you aren't covered, this will be priority number one. If you have a job lined up directly after high school / college and it provides health insurance, establishing and understanding your coverage will be explained in the upcoming section, under "Setting Up Your Employee Benefits." If there is a waiting (probation/grace) period before you qualify for employee benefits or your job prospects are limited and you need health insurance immediately, you should ensure you have a short term medical policy at a minimum. My nephew's example should be a testament to the possibility/probability of a momentary lapse in judgment or rotten luck at the most inopportune time, jeopardizing your financial future.

This health insurance discussion is focused primarily on graduates moving directly into the workforce, but let's not forget about graduates heading off to college. Briefly, if you are heading off to college in the fall and are covered by your parents' insurance, make sure to ask about out-of-network coverage within that health plan. You are generally covered for emergency services with out-of-network care, but nonemergency visits and procedures may have restrictions. This may be more of a worry for your parents, but if this is the case, you will want to look into health service plans offered through the university. The student health plan can be an option as an add-on to parental coverage to provide in-network care while you are away at school. The cost differences between an in-network student health plan and an out-of-network work plan can be substantial.

For those of you looking for gap coverage prior to employee benefits kicking in or for full individual coverage owing to limited or nonexistent parental health insurance, I encourage you to visit HealthCare.gov to get coverage quotes. You may be sent to a state website depending on state of residence. Nonetheless, be prepared to see your phone ring within seconds of hitting "Submit." While researching, I received three calls within five minutes (it's freaky fast without the sandwich). Get the quotes sent to you via e-mail to review with your parents or another trusted advisor. It doesn't hurt to get a quote to compare against your employer coverage once you secure employment and benefits. You will probably be hard pressed to find health insurance cheaper than the plan offered through your employer, especially if they are paying the lion's share of the premiums, but it doesn't hurt to double-check.

How Much Would Coverage Cost?

Good question. To give you an example of the expected monthly costs (policies quoted below are for three-month gap policies, not Obamacare), I used Minneapolis as the current residence and entered a single eighteen-year-old male with no preexisting conditions and no tobacco use. The costs range from $74 to $171 per month, depending on deductible, coinsurance, and annual maximum out of pocket expense. The idea is to obviously get the most coverage at the lowest cost but they (the healthcare industry) surely don't make it easy and keep in mind, this is only a three-month bridge policy to get you to a job that offers better coverage, at a much lower cost. Here is the breakdown for the $74 and $171 per month plan to show you what to expect.

$74 Plan:

- $5,000 deductible (this is what you would need to pay before the insurance would kick in).
- 30% coinsurance (you would need to cover the first $5,000 then 30% of cost thereafter, up to maximum out of pocket expense).
- Max out of pocket of $10,000 (you pay up to this amount, including deductible, then insurance would cover the rest) up to $750,000. $10,000 is the most you could pay for the year during a catastrophic event. Beware, all numbers reset annually on January 1st.

$171 Plan:

- $1,000 deductible (this is what you would need to pay before the insurance would kick in).
- 0% coinsurance. You pay the deductible and the insurance covers the rest up to the annual maximum of $1,500,000. They're betting that you'll never use this policy because of your age.
- Max out of pocket happens to be the same as the deductible in this policy, because the premiums are so high. Once the deductible is covered (by you) then insurance would cover the rest up to $1,500,000. And again, these numbers reset annually.

If you're healthy, take the higher deductible and lower coinsurance (as long as your cash reserve can cover the deductible). You want to keep costs low and hedge against a catastrophic injury or illness, which at your age, should be highly unlikely.

Make sure to check the fine print to determine if there are pre-existing condition restrictions that make the policy worthless. This means, beware of policies that won't cover health issues that you may be afflicted with now or in the past. Also, if you don't anticipate getting employer health benefits soon, make sure the prospective gap policy can be renewed beyond three months. Most states have different rules on this. Let me be the first to apologize for our shitty healthcare system in the United States. My advice: get a good job with benefits and remove this added stress.

If you don't have the income to pay for coverage, you may still have options through the Affordable Care Act. You may qualify for subsidies depending on your state of residence or Medicaid if you have no income. I'd go into more detail on this, but the landscape is ever evolving and the current administration is constantly looking to overhaul the health insurance program. My biggest fear is that your eyes are about to glaze over, you're on the verge of putting this book down and never picking it up again, due to overwhelming boredom. Just get the damn health insurance by visiting HealthCare.gov or search for short-term gap policies. Without health insurance, you may as well throw this book in the trash, because nothing else will matter if you get sick or injured.

I will provide additional information on health insurance terminology and what to look for in a policy in a later section, but I want to establish the foundation elements at a high level before diving deeper.

Now that you've verified that you have health insurance under your parents' plan or established a gap policy, let's move on to your cash reserve. This is an added level of protection to prevent your becoming a debt statistic.

Cash Reserve

According to a 2017 article reported on CBS Money Watch, 57 percent of Americans wouldn't be able to cover a $500 emergency expense without going into debt. That number completely astounded me. My wife and I have experienced two such emergencies in the past three years. Our dog Sasha ate six pair of my wife's underwear and one pair of socks. We didn't realize it at the time, because we were expecting our daughter and were a bit preoccupied. This little stunt resulted in an emergency visit to the veterinary hospital on a Sunday (of course), which amounted to a $3,700 emergency-surgery bill. You'll be happy to know that she's back to her old self, rummaging through our office trash and eating full rolls of toilet paper whenever we leave a door slightly ajar. The second expense was a bit more conventional: a nineteen-year-old hot-water heater had heated its last drop and needed replacing, lest it continue leaking all over our basement floor and pumping rusty sludge through our faucets. This was an additional $1,037 (pretty specific I know, just keeping it real) and happened exactly three weeks after the intestinal extraction (gross, I know). The point of this personal illustration is that shit happens—or in the case of my dog Sasha, doesn't happen. Get it? She couldn't poop because of the blockage. Sorry, no more poop jokes. We had built up an emergency fund, so we paid the bills with our Delta perks credit card, got the equivalent miles, and paid the card off in full the following day. We then backfilled the emergency fund.

What do you think of when I write the words "cash reserve"? Why do I ask you questions when I'm going to answer them anyway? If something is held in reserve, it isn't used immediately and is meant to be used when needed. This may be more commonly known as an emergency fund. The phrases are nearly synonymous, and I will use them interchangeably throughout this discussion.

A cash reserve is an account or series of accounts that hold roughly six months of your essential monthly living expenses to be used in the case of an emergency, such as a job loss, your car breaking down, or if you're a homeowner, your furnace or hot-water heater conking out. The emergency fund allows you to use cash instead of using credit cards or borrowing money from friends or family. This is meant to keep you out of debt.

Essential living expenses are just that, essential to your survival, and will be explained in more detail (with examples) in the budget section as you continue to read. For single wage earners, the equivalent of six months of essentials is deemed an appropriate level of reserves to withstand a job loss or another event that could cause financial hardship. Think about it. You strike out on your own, you have rent, a car payment (against my judgment), gas, electric, phone, Internet, and cable, and don't forget about food, and BAM—you lose your job. What do you do? At your age, you may be inclined to ask Mom and Dad for help. What if you don't have that option, or better yet, what if you choose not to saddle your parents with that responsibility? By establishing the cash reserve, you'll have the ability to take care of yourself. Without a proper cash reserve, you could find yourself trying to dig out from a mountain of high-interest credit-card debt for years.

Generally, I tell young people not to worry about where their cash reserves are invested, especially in this interest rate environment (cash is receiving virtually no interest). The idea is to have these accounts available immediately, which typically means a bank savings or checking account. Local-bank saving accounts are offering interest rates from 0.1 percent up to the highest I've found, 1 percent. That means that if you save $1,000 this year, you'll earn anywhere from $1 to $10 for the entire year. That's pathetic, but don't worry about it; just save it so you don't have to pay a credit card company 20 percent to borrow that same $1,000 and pay them $200 for the year in return.

For more investment savvy individuals, which you will be after reading this book, you can use a tiered reserve to provide levels of liquidity (accessibility) and attempt to gain a higher rate of return on the second and third tiers of your emergency fund. Don't become overwhelmed with the following. I just want to throw this concept out there and revisit it later. The more times you hear it, the more it will begin to sink in. The second tier can be a certificate of deposit (CD) or a cash-reserve certificate, which has less liquidity but a higher projected rate of return. Lastly, you could use a mutual fund or Exchange Traded Fund (ETF) as your third tier. I personally recommend a Roth IRA as your third tier of cash reserve. This is a retirement account first and foremost, but it is also the only retirement account that makes the contributions available for an emergency need without penalty or loan payments. To clarify, you can always take the contributions out of the Roth IRA without penalty; you just can't remove the interest or gains from the account without penalty prior to turning fifty-nine and a half (there are some hardship provisions, as well as education and first-time home-buyer allowances, but that is beyond the scope of this discussion).

That just got real confusing, didn't it? Your head is probably spinning from too many terms that are unfamiliar to you. Take a deep breath, throw some cold water on your face and press on. Again, we'll talk more about mutual funds, ETFs and Roth IRAs in the "Workplace Retirement Plan" and "Investing" sections.

We'll talk more about saving in several of the later sections once we've identified what your budget will be and how much is available to save in your cash-reserve fund. In addition to the cash-reserve savings, I've included a section on investing for short-term goals and, finally, the ultimate goal of retirement, albeit a ways off but equally important to consider, even at your age. So where is this money to cover expenses and fill your cash-reserve fund going to come from? A job, you say? Damn, you're smart!

Your First Full-Time Job

A cash reserve is tough to build and maintain without steady cash flow, and for most of you, that means your first full-time job. The time commitment of a job is very similar to that of school, when you think about it. You're essentially spending eight to nine hours a day away from home, but instead of listening to a teacher, you're providing a service or making something that can be sold for revenue. You have goals that you'll be asked to achieve, similar to grades that were required for you to progress in school. The key difference is that you now get paid for your time rather than your parents paying the school for your time. That's where the loose similarities end.

It can be a scary time, walking into a new place of employment, especially if you don't know anyone. One of the best pieces of advice I received on the eve of my first day on the job was to find the biggest coworker in the workplace and kick his/her ass. Let 'em know you're not going to take shit from no one! Nope, that's not right, my bad, that's if you're sent to prison. Scratch that advice, or turn to page 100, where I talk about what to do if you're sent to prison.

Don't feel bad. I would have checked to see if there was a page 100 too. I was kidding of course, you kick anyone's ass at work and you're fired, end of story. Had to make sure you were still paying attention.

All right, first day of work—what should you expect? You've got roughly 11,421 days of work ahead of you, so I hope you picked the right career path. Actually, research indicates that individuals average 3.8 years in a job (from the *Wall Street Journal*). I've had twelve jobs at last count, and I've got nearly fifteen years of work life left.

OK, enough statistics. You finally get an opportunity to earn some real money and do with it as you please. Whether that first job is a professional position that requires a suit and tie, a trade position in which you carry a tool belt, or a service position that requires you to wear a uniform, chances are that if this is a full-time position, you'll be offered benefits. I'll take this opportunity to plug the importance of those benefits. Take full advantage, since they are an extension of your pay. If you didn't have employee benefits, you'd be getting a higher wage and forced to go elsewhere to secure insurance, so you want to make sure you're maximizing these, but only the benefits that are right for your situation. I'll go into more detail on this in a future section devoted to maximizing benefits. This section is devoted to understanding your paycheck and deciphering how your pay is calculated and what deductions will affect your take-home (net) pay. With this information, we'll put together a budget and give you an idea of what to expect as you strike out on your own.

Breaking Down Your Pay Stub

Depending on your employer, you may get paid every two weeks (twenty-six paychecks per year) or twice monthly (twenty-four paychecks per year). For the purposes of this book, I've assumed a biweekly paycheck (twenty-six paychecks over a full calendar year). This can be confusing because your budget is typically calculated monthly and that's what I've done here. Stay with me.

For this example and ease of explanation, I've assumed a first full year of wages at $31,200, or $15 per hour over forty hours per week, for fifty-two weeks (even though as a recent graduate you may only be working a partial year). For some of you, $31,200 annually may be a stretch; for others, this will be way too low. Regardless, it doesn't change my advice or this example conceptually.

For those of you who are looking at a pay stub for the very first time, I don't want you to be alarmed. It will be lower than you expect, but it's good to come to this realization before you start planning out how much rent, car payment (again, against my better judgment), and other lifestyle expenses you can afford. What is taken out of your paycheck can be shocking at first, until you understand where everything is going. To be clear, you won't receive the full $1,200 biweekly (twenty-six pay periods), owing to taxes and other deductions from employee benefits (once established), such as health, dental, vision, life and disability insurance, potentially a 401(k) contribution, and so on.

Let's start with the taxes, namely state and federal income tax, which you are probably familiar with. There is a less known tax called FICA, which stands for Federal Insurance Contributions Act. FICA tax is a combination of Social Security and Medicare tax and is the only flat tax that we'll talk about. By flat, I mean it's a set percentage for all income levels and is not spread across marginal tax brackets like federal and state taxes are (this may seem confusing, but we'll break these down in a few minutes).

You've probably heard your parents complain about taxes from time to time. Well, guess what: now you can experience the joy of taxes for yourself. The government needs to assess taxes to pay for the services that we take for granted. Taxes, whether they come from income, property, or sales tax, pay for police, fire departments, school districts, road maintenance, and the like. In other words, taxes, as you should know from your civics class or similar, provide the quality of life we've come to expect in America.

Before the government can assess tax from your salary, that salary is reduced by what we call pretax deductions, such as the insurance premiums and 401(k) contributions (except those to Roth 401(k)s, which are posttax contributions) I alluded to earlier. Let's assume you have the opportunity to establish your health, life, and disability insurance through your employer. This is an awesome benefit and one that shouldn't be taken lightly. This will help establish that critical foundation I talked about earlier, and the beauty of it is, your employer is going to pay the lion's share of it. We'll talk about the insurance coverage to select in the upcoming sections; what we're concerned with here are how those deductions affect your cash flow. I've put together a sample (so simple it may have looked better in crayon) of deductions to demonstrate the impact on cash flow. Your benefit dollar amounts will vary, but the concepts are valid.

Income	$ 1,200.00
Medical	$ 61.93
Dental	$ 11.93
Vision	$ 2.63
Net selary after pre-tax deductions	$ 1,123.51

You have $1,200 of income for two weeks of work ($15/hour × 80 hours). The big three—medical, dental, and vision—amount to 6.4 percent of your pay taken right off the top (in this example). You'll notice that the medical expense is huge. Yep, but the alternative is a hell of a lot worse. There are options for reducing this amount, and those will be discussed in the benefits section.

After the employee benefit deductions, you're left with $1,123.51. Next, we'll look at the impact of federal and state income tax on your remaining net salary.

Federal taxes are determined through what is known as a marginal tax bracket. The IRS couldn't make this easy, so they have different levels of income taxed at different brackets. In 2018, for a single tax filer, which you presumably are, you will pay $952.50 on the first $9,525 of income that you earn (this is the 10 percent bracket). You will then pay 15 percent tax on the difference between $29,211 ($31,200 reduced by 26 pay periods of pretax deductions = $29,211) and that first $9,525 ($31,200 − $1,989 − $9,525 = $19,686). So, 0.15 times $19,686 equals $2,952.90 in tax. Add these two taxes together, and that is your total federal tax obligation ($2,952.90 + $952.50 = $3,905.40). Divide $3,905.40 by 26 (the number of pay periods), and your biweekly federal income tax will equate to $150.20 per paycheck (in this example). These numbers may be different owing to the tax withholdings/allowances you selected when you set up your W-4 (tax information/worksheet filled out when you start your new job) and personal exemptions (covered in the "Filing Your First Tax Return" section). **Note:** a higher number of tax withholdings allow you to keep more of your paycheck but potentially open you up to a tax bill when you file your tax return in April of the following year. Leave your withholdings at 1 for now.

That's your federal tax obligation. Each state is a little different as to how they assess state income tax, and some states don't actually assess an income tax, such as Alaska, Texas, Nevada, South Dakota, Florida, Tennessee, and New Hampshire.

For the state of Minnesota, where our fictional income is derived, we have a marginal tax bracket again, and for 2018, it would break down like this:

The first $25,890 of income will be taxed at 5.35 percent, which equates to $1,385.12. Then, the difference between your $29,211 ($31,200 reduced by pretax deductions) and the $25,890 is $3,321, and that will be taxed at 7.05 percent, which equates to $234.13 in additional tax. Add the two for your annual Minnesota state income tax ($1,385.12 + $234.13) of $1,619.25. Divide that by the 26 pay periods, and you have $62.28 of state income tax per paycheck (in this example)

Now for the final tax, FICA, otherwise known as payroll tax. FICA is broken down to Social Security and Medicare tax. The Social Security portion of the payroll tax is 6.20 percent. In our example, the tax is assessed on the remaining income after pretax deductions. So, our $1,123 × 0.062 = $69.63. The Medicare tax is 1.45 percent, so $1,123 × 0.0145 = $16.28. The total FICA tax of 7.65 percent equates to $85.91 (shown below).

Income after deductions	$ 1,123.51
Tax deductions	
Federal tax	$ 150.20
State tax	$ 62.28
FICA tax	$ 85.91
Net Income after tax	$ 825.12

Now that we've reduced your income by pretax employee benefits and taxes, there is still the matter of after-tax deductions. In this case we've decided to contribute to a Roth 401(k) because of your relatively low tax bracket and high earning potential. We'll talk about this contribution and the justification for it in a future discussion under the "Workplace Retirement Plan" section. We also have an after-tax (posttax) disability insurance deduction.

I've assumed an employer matching contribution of 5 percent (a great benefit), so you want to make sure that you are taking full advantage and contribute 5 percent of your own money, posttax, into the Roth 401(k) option. Your 5 percent contribution is deducted from your paycheck posttax and is based on the gross (total) income value of $31,200, so per paycheck, you'll see a $60 contribution ($1,200 x .05). In this example, you put in $60 per paycheck and your company matches $60 per paycheck. That really builds over time. As a note, if you were contributing into a traditional 401(k), you would see 5 percent of your paycheck show up in the pretax deductions along with the medical/dental/vision premiums before the federal and state income taxes were assessed.

Again, I will go over my justification for you contributing posttax rather than pretax, due to your age and income level, in the "Workplace Retirement Plan" section. **The key takeaway**; no matter your retirement plan options, contribute the percentage required to receive the full employer matching contribution.

Lastly, the disability insurance premium is depicted as a posttax deduction in this example. If you have the option to select a pretax or posttax disability insurance premium, select the posttax option. In the event of a prolonged injury or illness, in which you are unable to work, the benefit will be paid to you tax-free (we'll talk about disability insurance in the benefits section).

Net income	$ 825.12
Post-tax deductions	
Disability	$ 5.11
Roth 401{k}	$ 60.00
Income remaining after all deductions	$ 760.01

Congratulations, you have roughly $1,647 per month ($760 × 26 pay periods divided by 12 months) to cover expenses, additional savings and fun stuff. Again, this is confusing because you have $760 of net income per paycheck but you are not getting paid twice monthly, you're getting paid every two weeks or what they call bi-weekly (26 vs. 24 pay periods). You'll have two months that you'll receive a third paycheck. I hope that makes more sense and you now know why I've used the $1,647 of net income per month instead of the $1,520 per month. How far will that $1,647 per month get you? Good question.

Your Budget

Now that you know how your income is carved up, it seems only logical to talk about how this will affect your budget. At its core, the budget is a pretty easy concept to understand. You shouldn't spend more than you earn; otherwise, you accrue debt and pay someone else interest for however long you hold that debt. This is one of the biggest temptations that I will continuously tell you to avoid, especially consumer debt, such as credit cards. Credit cards are evil, and should be required by law to display skull and crossbones on the front of every card.

Debt is only one of the potential expenses that will affect your budget. You'll have essential expenses that must be paid every month, such as rent, groceries, car payment (don't do it), electricity, and gas for heating and cooking—in other words, the necessities of life. These are the expenses you heard me talk about when I discussed your cash-reserve goal amount. In addition to the essentials, are the lifestyle or discretionary expenses that are crucial not for your survival but your sanity. These are expenses for your phone, cable television, Internet, eating out, daily coffee, cigarettes (I hope not), and travel, to name a few. If an expense needs to be reduced or eliminated to free up money for savings, this is the bucket that will suffer. I've projected the expenses below to illustrate living in a very small studio apartment or with a roommate to keep costs a bit lower. Many of these reflect reality but may not be all inclusive. Cost of living will be substantially different across the country, but again, the concepts are still relevant, whether you live in Seattle or Bangor (that's in Maine, in case you struggle with geography).

The point to focus on is that your money may not go as far as you think and you may have to reduce or eliminate some costs to accomplish that cash reserve we discussed. You may have some leeway with the car payment too. As we'll see, there are a few options for getting from point A to point B, and depending on your preference, you could free up dollars here to direct toward goals or other priorities. Now, if you forego a car altogether, those car-payment dollars may go away, but you will experience increased public transportation expenses for cabs, buses, Lift or Uber. You'll save on gas, tolls, and parking as well, but you get the picture. You want to set a budget and make sure you have dollars to save, to establish those six months of living expenses for your cash-reserve goal.

Essential Expenses:	
Pay Yourself First	?
Rent	$ 400
Renter's Insurance	$ 10
Car Payment	$ 250
Car Insurance	$ 70
Gas	$ 60
Groceries	$ 100
Utilities	$ 60
Total Essentials	**$ 950**

Discretionary Expenses:	
Phone	$ 80
Internet	$ 20
Cable TV	$ 50
Dining Out	$ 100
Entertainment	$ 60
Gym Membership	$ 30
Daily Coffee	$ 80
Clothes Purchases	$ 50

Total Discretionary	$ 470
Monthly Net Income ($ 760 x 26) divided by 12 months	**$ 1,647**
Total Expenses	**$ 1,420**
Surplus	**$ 227**

From this example, you've got $227 per month to save toward your cash-reserve goal on a monthly basis. Keep in mind that you won't see that surplus every month, but there will be two months when you will receive a third paycheck because you are getting paid every two weeks (in this example).

The essential expenses that make up your cash-reserve goal amount are rent, utilities (gas and electric), renter's insurance, car payment, car insurance (assuming you stay on your parent's plan for lower costs), gas for your car, and groceries. These total $950 per month. Multiply that by six months, and you have $5,700. Therefore, the cash-reserve goal you are saving for is $5,700. By saving $227 per month, it would take you twenty-five months to accomplish the cash-reserve goal. That's a little over two years, which isn't terrible, but could be better. I suggest that you free up more savable dollars per month. How do you accomplish this? Something must be eliminated, right? Your precious cell phone isn't getting cut. You've got to eat. How about... your car payment of $250 per month? What if you continued driving that piece-of-crap used car that your parents gave you in high school? You know, the one you parked miles from the high school parties so you wouldn't be noticed getting out of said piece of crap. That embarrassment is going to save you an additional $200 per month ($50 assumed for used-car maintenance per month) and shorten that emergency-fund-savings-goal completion date to thirteen months, and that's awesome! The other thing you have going for you are potential raises, tax refunds, or performance bonuses that could be used to shorten the savings period even more. Again, this is only one example of cuts that could be made. You'll need to assess your priorities, and I don't care how you come up with the money (short of knocking off a liquor store or selling a kidney), just come up with the monthly cash flow to establish that emergency fund.

Cash Reserve (Revisited)

Now that you know that you're shooting for a cash-reserve goal of $5,700 and that you have potentially $447 to save monthly (without the car payment), this is your *"pay yourself first"* money.

What does it mean to pay yourself first? You pay yourself a set dollar amount every month ($447 in this example) as if it were another essential expense.

This should be set up as a systematic savings from your checking account into your savings account. It's pretty simple, really, and will protect you from your whimsical purchases in your day-to-day life.

As you begin accumulating savings, you can break your cash-reserve balance of $5,700 (your dollar amount will be different) into this three-tier structure:

- 20 percent in your checking/savings account
- 30 percent in a cash reserve certificate or high yield savings account (beware of account costs)
- 50 percent in a Roth IRA (this is different than your Roth 401(k))

Once your cash reserve is fully established, you can look to allocate that freed-up $447 per month toward a new savings goal, such as buying a newer car, taking a trip, or saving for a down payment on a house.

Make sure to double check savings and brokerage account fees in the small print to ensure your interest rate isn't completely eaten up by account fees. If it isn't apparent, call and ask what the fees are specifically. Also, ask if there are hidden fees such as account closure fees. Shop around to find the highest rate of return on cash while keeping account fees as low as possible.

All right, let's check in on your progress. You've established your health insurance, cash reserve, and budget. What's next? Well I'll tell you. Establishing the remainder of your employee benefits. We've touched on this topic from time to time in previous sections but haven't devoted sufficient time to the topic itself. I want to make sure you establish protection for your health, vision (if applicable), dental, disability, and life through your employer if available. You may as well defer as many costs to your employer as possible. Buckle up, this is going to get exciting!!

Chapter 3

Setting Up Your Employee Benefits

I WANT TO MAKE sure that you are fully capitalizing on your employee benefits through work. As I stated earlier, these benefits are an extension of your pay and should be considered lost money if you are not maximizing this opportunity. I'll warn you that the benefits booklet will be excruciatingly long and boring, but with this guide, you should be able to go to the relevant sections and pick the coverage that is right for you. This is important to get right the first time because you'll have an opportunity to make selections when you're first hired but not again until late in the fall during a one- or two-week period called the open enrollment period. You typically get one crack at this for the year, so let's make it worthwhile.

To be sure, not every company is going to offer the same level of benefits. A large corporation like Apple, Pepsi, Google, or General Motors is typically going to provide better benefits than Burt's Plastic and Molding Corp. Just be thankful that you're getting benefits. Many who earn a wage fend for their own health, vision, dental, and retirement plans through an external wholesaler for a much higher cost or, unfortunately, do without.

The first thing you'll want to do is determine whether you are immediately eligible for benefits. Some companies may require that you pass a probation period to determine whether you are worthy of extending these benefits to. It costs money to set up benefits for a new employee, and many companies won't want to waste their time or money on an employee who won't be there in sixty to ninety days. Once this probation period has lapsed, you should be able to enjoy the benefits you've established.

Whether there's a probation period or not doesn't change the importance of selecting the right benefits when you're first hired. When I read my first employee-benefits booklet, I was overwhelmed by the sheer size of the document and all the corporate acronyms and abbreviations, which undoubtedly made perfect sense to the human resources professional who put the stupid document together but not to a recent grad. Don't get caught up in the corporate speak. Look through the table of contents, and search for these headers: Health Insurance or Medical Plan, Vision, Dental, Prescription Drugs, Disability, Life Insurance, and Retirement Plan or the equivalent represented by the strange numbers 401(k)/403(b). If you have questions, ask! Don't be timid and miss out on something just because you were afraid to speak up.

Let's start with the granddaddy of them all, health insurance. Look for this section in your employee-benefits PDF, booklet, or binder. As we discussed earlier, this is the most important of the foundation cornerstones and therefore is by far the most important component of your employee-benefits package as well. You will be deferring a huge cost to your employer and protecting yourself against an industry that can ruin you financially with one prolonged illness or injury. I've addressed the terminology below, as well as what to expect from your first visit to the doctor to the nitty gritty of receiving the bill in the mail.

Health Insurance

This section is meant to give you a clear understanding of the terminology when you make your plan selection and, in general, how the health-care process works from the time you arrive at your first appointment to the time you are billed for that appointment. Keep in mind that every health-care plan will be slightly different, but most of the concepts are the same. My hope is that this will alleviate anxiety when you are thinking about health care.

The terminology and numbers illustrated below are consistent with employer-sponsored coverage, but the terminology extends to individual policies through a private provider as well. Your plan will have different rates.

- *Premium:* This is the dollar amount that you'll pay from each of your paychecks and is paid pretax (for work policies). You'll see this listed on your pay stub every two weeks (some twice monthly). The size of your employer, level of services provided and the number of employees participating in the health insurance plan will dictate how expensive your monthly cost will be. Health insurance parameters will play a part in the cost of your monthly premium as well (see below for more on this). Note: The overall premium is much higher than the dollar amount you are paying per pay period. Your employer typically pays the lion's share of this monthly bill. So, pat your CEO on the back the next time you see him or her and say, "Thanks, buddy." Then prepare to be walked off the premises for touching the CEO.

- *In-network:* Most health insurance plans will ask you to stay within a network of doctors with whom they have contracted for specific rates. This allows the insurance company to manage its costs and avoid outlandish fees from unknown providers. If you already have a family doctor, you'll need to check to see whether he/she is in the network of approved providers or find a doctor that is.
- *Out-of-network:* To expand on the "in-network" explanation above, this is a doctor that is not listed in the network of negotiated doctors and therefore can still typically be used but will cost additional dollars monthly. I do not recommend this option. This may have to be used in an emergency however, when on a trip, for example.
- *Copay:* With many health insurance plans, you'll have to pay a copay, which is a fee for every visit to the doctor's office. This is typically between ten and twenty-five dollars per visit.
- *Deductible:* This is the amount of out-of-pocket dollars that you may have to pay before your true health insurance coverage kicks in. Depending on your plan, the deductible may be a few hundred dollars up to a couple thousand, if the company is small and is spreading the cost over fewer participants. Typically, your copays will go against this deductible amount. So, each time you visit the doctor's office and pay the copay of twenty dollars, you've reduced your deductible by that twenty dollars. **The deductible resets every calendar year**.
- *Coinsurance:* Once the deductible is met, all future visits (within the calendar year) and resulting expenses will be covered at a certain percentage. For most plans that I've seen, the insurance company will cover 80 percent of the future costs, and you will be responsible for the remaining 20 percent up to a maximum out-of-pocket for the year (see below). For example, if you have paid your entire deductible for the year and have incurred another $1,000 in medical bills, you would have to pay $200, and the insurance company would pay the remaining $800.
- *Maximum out of pocket:* In the previous example, it still seems as if you're paying a lot of money, since you are also paying monthly premiums for this insurance while you may not be visiting the doctor. The maximum out of pocket is the savior. This protects you from catastrophic expenses incurred by an accident or long-term stays in the hospital. The insurance company sets a maximum dollar amount that you are responsible for in a calendar year. This may be anywhere from $2,000 up to $5,000 or $10,000, depending on the amount of plan participants. For instance, let's say you were riding your mountain bike and wiped out and punctured a lung or had a head injury and were required to stay in the hospital for several weeks. You could be looking at a $100,000+ medical bill without insurance. With a maximum out-of-pocket expense of, say, $5,000, you'd pay the

$5,000, and the insurance company would pick up the rest of the tab. It doesn't take a genius to realize that $5,000 in medical debt is easier to overcome than $100,000 or several hundred thousand.

One of the most important things to keep in mind is that **all these costs will reset every calendar year.** That means any dollars you have paid against your deductible will start over at zero beginning on January 1 of the following year. The same goes for maximum out-of-pocket expenses. Thinking strategically about doctor's visits if you have already met (paid) the deductible for the year and still need follow-up visits. You will want to cram those in before the end of the year if at all possible, before the meter resets.

At your age, every dollar counts. OK, at nearly every age, every dollar counts. Here are tips to reduce your monthly premium costs:

- If you are healthy and don't plan to visit the doctor's office more than once a year for a physical, you could increase your deductible to the highest available. So instead of a $250 deductible, you may increase it to $1,000. You're betting against the insurance company that you won't spend more than a copay and the cost of a physical. This could save you $5 or $10 per paycheck, which translates to a savings of $130 to $260 per year. Now keep in mind that a couple of visits to the doctor or a broken arm in one calendar year will make you regret choosing the higher deductible. The higher deductible should be chosen only if you have your cash reserve established (the second corner of your foundation). There may be a health savings account (HSA) option as well, which will be described in detail a bit later, which is a great opportunity if you are healthy.
- Choose a plan that provides reduced-cost coverage for in-network care. You may have the ability to choose a health plan that is out of network to continue seeing your family doctor for an additional cost. By choosing the in-network list of clinics, you can save dollars every paycheck as well. Choose a new doctor, and save the dollars every month. The savings from choosing in-network care and increasing your deductible may save you a few hundred dollars annually, and this money can be applied to your cash reserve or if fully established, a down payment on a house.

Health Savings Account (HSA)

There is one other health plan that I want to bring to your attention and could make a lot of sense for a young, healthy individual. This plan is called a health savings account, or HSA. Not all plans will offer this option, but if it is offered, you should consider it, especially if you are healthy, single and especially if your employer provides a matching contribution.

The HSA is available only if you choose the high-deductible option through your provider (considered a high-deductible plan) and that deductible is at least $1,350 per year. So, if you do incur medical costs throughout the year, you are going to pay a higher dollar amount out of pocket prior to the coinsurance kicking in. In other words, if your high-deductible option carries a deductible of $1,350, you'll pay all out-of-pocket costs up to that dollar amount before your insurance kicks in and covers 80 percent (or actual plan percentage), with you covering the remaining 20 percent. You may be thinking that that sounds like a terrible deal, but I haven't told you the benefits yet. The advantage of the HSA is that your monthly insurance premiums are less because you are assuming more risk. You have the ability to contribute dollars into the HSA, similar to a retirement account, that can be invested for long-term growth. The beauty is that the contributions are pretax, and if used for qualified medical expenses, those dollars are tax-free upon redemption. This is the best of both worlds. You get a tax break on the contributions, and taxes are not assessed on the back end either. This is the only investment that offers double preferential tax treatment. For 2018, you can contribute $3,450 per year into this account (for single tax filers). You may not have that amount of cash flow, but contribute what you can once your cash reserve and retirement plan contributions are fully established (depending on other short-term goals you may have).

Benefits of the HSA

- Tax-deductible contributions to an investment account
- Some employers offer matching contributions
- Tax-free redemptions from account if used for qualifying medical expenses
- Funds are available at any time if used for qualified medical expenses and have no age requirements for distributions, which are limitations of retirement accounts
- Lower insurance premiums (cost of insurance)
- Fully portable: If you leave your employer, you can roll this into a personal account (one caveat: matching contributions may not be fully vested/transferrable)

Limitations of the HSA

- High-deductible plan: If you are forced to visit the doctor more than originally expected, you will have to cover the higher deductible (out of pocket) before coinsurance kicks in

- Not offered by every plan

Your First Visit to the Doctor's Office

The first thing you'll need to do is choose your in-network clinic. You can get a list of clinics that qualify for your network from your plan provider's website, or call the service number on the back of your insurance card (provided by your health-care provider) and get a list of affiliated clinics. If you have a family doctor, you can ask whether that doctor is part of your in-network plan. This insurance card will be very important and should be kept in your wallet or purse wherever you go. Better yet, take a picture of the front and back of the card with your phone as a backup. Once you've picked your clinic, call that clinic, and schedule an appointment (only if you need to see a doctor, of course, but at least once per year for a physical). The clinic will ask you for the medical plan provider name, such as Medica or Blue Cross / Blue Shield or similar. Then they will ask for the plan identification number or group number. It will be spelled out on the card very clearly. Once you've given them the appropriate numbers, you can tell them that you don't have a doctor yet. One will be assigned to you. Keep in mind that there will usually be multiple doctors at the clinic, and if you are not comfortable with the assigned doctor, you can ask for another before the next visit. This may not seem like a big deal at the time, but you may be connected to this doctor for many years, so make sure you're not settling and take a few for a test drive.

On the day of the appointment, make sure to bring your insurance card and a form of payment if your plan requires a copay. Most clinics will take a photocopy of the card to keep on file and will ask you every time you come back whether your insurance information has changed. Having the card will save you time and hassle. If there is a required copay, it will typically be collected when you check in and may range from ten to twenty-five dollars. Depending on the clinic, they may not take a debit card, so bring some cash. One other thing you may be asked is whether you would like to sign up for MyCharts (may have a different name), which is a web-based health-record system that can be used to schedule future appointments, ask questions of the medical staff, and share appointment summaries and test results. This is a great service and a great way to interact with your clinic, so sign up. You will be notified via e-mail when your test results have been posted on the website.

After you've checked in for your nine o'clock appointment, prepare to sit and wait until nine thirty to be called; that's if your clinic is anything like mine. Once you are called and taken to an office, prepare to wait an additional fifteen minutes for the actual doctor to show up. It's the nature of the business, I'm afraid. We won't go into details on the exam; that's between you and your doctor.

If this is a routine visit for an annual physical or deemed general maintenance (health-care speak), you may not have to pay anything above and beyond the copay, but if this is a follow-up appointment for a sickness or injury, you will probably be on the hook for 100 percent up to the deductible amount before the coinsurance kicks in. You will receive a notice in the mail, an estimate of benefits (EOB) from your insurance company that will clearly state that "This is not a bill." This statement will explain what the visit cost and what portion your insurance covered (if any). This is simply a statement for your records. The actual bill will come from your clinic, explaining what you owe and payment instructions. Pay this on time from your checking account, or if you need to, tap into your cash reserve; that's why it's there. Don't put this on a credit card and assume you'll pay it later; you'll forget.

I know that seems like a lot of information, and until you've been through the experience, it may seem daunting, but it isn't—I promise.

Dental Plan

How much do you love getting your teeth cleaned? I hate it! The sound of metal scraping my enamel is enough to make my eyes water every time. How about the flossing at the dentist? Why do they have to ram the floss so deep into your gums? Aaargh! Nevertheless, it's another of life's necessities that should be done twice a year. If your employer offers this plan, take it and run. I pay $11.93 per paycheck ($310 per year), which may seem high, but if you consider the cost of uninsured preventive care, such as teeth cleanings, a potential cavity, or the worst experience possible, a root canal, this is a no-brainer.

You may have a few options to choose from, such as routine, traditional, and extended plans. Our routine plan covers the cost of two teeth cleanings a year, x-rays, and fillings (preventive care). The traditional plan covers the routine care plus crowns, bridges, and braces (orthodontics) for kids and adults. Extended coverage covers the traditional plus root canals (for my plan as an example). I hope you never have to experience a root canal, but if you know you have a need for one of the procedures listed in the traditional or extended plans, you should, obviously, sign up for those plans. Keep in mind that open enrollment happens only once per year for the very reason that insurance companies don't want you switching insurance coverages midyear owing to an expensive procedure coming up and your needing the insurance company to flip the majority of the bill. Plan according to need, especially if you are able to wait until open enrollment for the more expensive procedure. Keep in mind, however, that if open enrollment is in November, your new coverage won't be active until the first of the new year.

If you have healthy teeth and don't plan on getting punched in the mouth by some drunk idiot or chipping a tooth playing in some silly intramural basketball game, then opt for the routine plan and cut your costs in half; you may save yourself $100 or more annually.

For any of the non-preventive care procedures, you will have similar payment requirements as the medical coverage: deductibles, copays, and maximum benefits per year. This will be laid out in the dental-plan portion of your benefits booklet. I have never paid anything over the premiums during my fourteen-year span with my company, but then again, I've been fortunate.

Vision Plan

If you have good eyes and don't get a regular eye check every year (other than the eye chart at your annual doctor's appointment), skip this insurance and save yourself between $100 and $200 per year. You'll have the opportunity to pick up this coverage every year at open enrollment time, so if you feel you would like to get a vision check and may need corrective eyewear, then you can always sign up the next year, but save yourself this monthly expense. Vision coverage doesn't cover the cost of injuries or diseases of the eye, so don't worry; your health insurance will cover costs related to glaucoma, cataracts, losing an eyeball in a camping or Marlin fishing accident, or something as drastic as that.

If you already have corrective eyewear and typically get eye exams once a year or are interested in getting Lasik surgery, you may have a couple of options for this type of vision coverage (in many plans). My work plan offers basic and premium. Basic is $2.63 per paycheck ($68.38 per year), which is the coverage I have. I have never had glasses or contacts, so I have essentially spent nearly $1,000 (over fourteen years) and never had an eye exam. As alluded to above, if you already have glasses or may be looking for laser vision-correction surgery (Lasik), you may want to consider the premium package, which has premiums that are a little less than double the cost, at $4.47 per paycheck ($116.22 annually). Again, these numbers are strictly examples of my plan and could vary drastically from your numbers.

Vison has the same copay, deductible, and maximum benefits allowed per year as medical and dental, but the list of line-item costs is very specific as far as what is covered and what is not.

In summary, if you have good eyes, skip the coverage and build your cash reserve instead. If you have glasses or contacts already or have blurred vision right now, get the insurance and get an eye exam and use the insurance. If you have kids, get the insurance.

Disability-Income Insurance (DI)

You may not be familiar with disability insurance, but one thing will become abundantly clear now that you're transitioning to adulthood. There's insurance for everything: car, house, life, personal identity, health, rental, dental, and disability income, to name a few. There may be some in that list that you didn't even know existed and some that I addressed in previous sections. The overarching theme is that you want to protect everything of actual or perceived value against unforeseen events that could depreciate or completely wipe out that value. For example, car insurance has become a legal obligation imposed by most states owing to the financial hardship you could inflict on others. If you didn't hold this insurance, you wouldn't be able to compensate those individuals for their losses at your hands. You are required by law to hold liability insurance on your automobile (at a minimum). In the event you are involved in a car accident, are at fault, and inflict bodily injury on a passenger in your car or the other car or destroy property directly attributable to your negligence, you will have the ability to pay those affected. We as a society have become so litigious (lawsuit happy) that it has become increasingly important to protect ourselves as well as our property.

In this section, I want to discuss insuring your single most important asset: your ability to earn an income. If you think about the earning potential you have at this point in your life and career, the sky, truly, is the limit. The income possibilities are enormous, even for someone who is starting his/her first fifteen-dollar-per-hour job. Let's do the math on our fifteen-dollar-per-hour example. As you may have noticed, I like to put a monetary value on everything. Money gets people's attention; for better or worse, we are motivated by money, and everything becomes easier to understand and more relevant when monetized.

Let's say you don't make a dime more than that $15 per hour for the rest of your life. That's a ridiculous assumption but it's an easier calculation, so cut me some slack. Assuming a retirement age of sixty-eight (the next fifty years, for easy math), you're looking at $1.56 million in income over that fifty-year period. That's a hell of a lot of income, and frankly, that's if you're a pretty bad employee and don't receive one single pay increase over those fifty years.

So, what happens to that income if you get sick or get into a car accident, get hurt skiing, run into a tree on your bike, fall off a cliff that's high enough to severely hurt you but not kill you, or countless other examples? If you can't work, you don't get paid, right? If you were to ask someone on the street, "Who will take care of you if you can't work and earn a wage?" most would reply, "The government" or "My family." The government may begrudgingly take care of you as a last resort, but the care provided will be dictated by them. Family members will probably take care of you if they can afford to do so, but think of the financial and emotional strain on them. There is another option, called disability insurance, that can help bridge the income gap if you become too sick or injured to work.

As I stated before, there is an insurance product for everything. You wouldn't think twice about insuring your car or house with values of thousands to hundreds of thousands of dollars. What about something that is worth $1.5 million over your lifetime?

How Does Disability Insurance Work?

Many, if not most, large corporate employers will offer some sort of disability-income insurance, and it is based on a percentage of your income. There are two types of disability insurance, which are really based on two different timeframes. You'll have short-term disability (STD, an unfortunate acronym), which is generally ninety days of 100 percent income replacement, and then, you guessed it, long-term disability (LTD), which picks up after the ninety-day STD (again, unfortunate, but one of the only STDs that runs out after ninety days) has run out. The long-term coverage will generally be in the neighborhood of 50–66 percent. So, if you are making our example of $31,200 per year and have LTD insurance coverage of 66 percent and get hit by a car, you would receive $20,592 per year, generally until age sixty-seven (consensus retirement age for someone of your generation). Your employer won't offer you 100 percent coverage beyond the short term, or you would have no incentive to come back to work. Let's be honest: there are a lot of people out there that would abuse the system, fake an injury or sickness, and sit back and collect disability income until retirement.

That $20,592 of income is fully taxable in most cases, just as your annual salary of $31,200 is. This reduced sum of money isn't going to allow you to live as you were before the disability, but it is going to allow you to eat and have a place to sleep at night. If a company gives you the option for disability benefits, take it and pay the four to six dollars per paycheck to have the maximum coverage they offer. If the company gives you the option to pay for the disability coverage with after-tax dollars, take it and smile. With the after-tax premiums, if you become disabled, your $20,592 will actually amount to the full $20,592 and will not be taxed, because you paid the monthly premium with after-tax dollars.

There are insurance companies that offer an individual disability-income policy (above and beyond your work insurance) that will allow you to pick up an additional 15–20 percent of coverage, but instead of paying four to six dollars for 66 percent, you'll pay maybe twenty to forty dollars per month for the additional coverage (depending on occupation, age, insurability, and policy benefits). That add-on individual policy will be paid to you tax-free as well. This may be a luxury you can't afford at this time, but as you continue to increase your income and have a wife/husband and kids, you will want to protect that additional 15–20 percent of income, especially if you are the sole earner in the relationship and your livelihood depends on your income.

Some may say, "Why pay for coverage when you can rely on social security disability?" Those people haven't tried to get social security disability. It's hard to qualify, and most times you'll be denied several times before your claim is accepted. Let's say it takes two years before your claim is accepted and processed. You'll be compensated back to the original date of submission, but in the meantime, you've racked up two years' worth of debt. Get the cheap group (employer-sponsored) disability coverage for the maximum percentage offered, paid with after-tax dollars if possible, and if you have the cash flow for the individual disability policy, get that too. This is a necessary evil because, again, this is your biggest asset.

Skeptics may still say, "My family will help if I'm disabled." Have you talked to your family to determine whether they are willing to continue working throughout their retirement to support your needs? Don't make this decision for them and assume they'll be happy with it; that's selfish. Pay the extra four to six dollars per month to provide some support to your family, who will still probably be caring for you, but at least they'll have an additional $20,592 to put toward your care. If nothing else, they can buy life insurance with your disability-income paycheck to provide for you after they pass on.

There are other components to individual disability insurance that you should be aware of before you purchase that additional individual policy, such as waiting periods, the type of occupation the insurance will cover, coverage periods for different occupations, integration with social security, and so on. That is something you should talk to a financial advisor about prior to getting additional coverage.

Life Insurance

I'm assuming you're single if you are graduating from high school this year, and that assumption carries considerable weight when determining your life insurance need. Life insurance is typically needed to provide for a spouse, a child, or a business partner in the event you pass away prematurely. It's never a pleasant thing to think about but should be a priority when you have one of the individuals identified above to worry about. Since you are presumably single, with no kids, and are not a part owner in a business currently, this shouldn't be a huge priority, and I don't recommend getting anything more than what may be free through your employer. At many companies, you may be able to get one times your annual income free (up to $50,000) or at a very reasonable rate. This will provide your loved ones with the financial means to cover your funeral and burial and not cause them financial hardship in addition to their emotional distress.

You may have been told by friends or read conflicting blog posts saying that your family will incur debt that you leave behind. This isn't true unless your friends and family have cosigned for something or undertaken that debt with you. Creditors (companies you owe money to) will make a claim against your estate to pay off any debt owed, but that debt and the terms of that debt aren't transferred to your heirs (unless cosigned).

If you have talked with an insurance agent, financial advisor, or similar, and he/she has tried to pitch an insurance product to you, ask yourself this question: Why do I need this insurance? If you are young and healthy and don't have anyone depending on you, you don't need life insurance above and beyond what I described above (final expenses). The person pitching the insurance is paid a commission from the sale of that product, and may have a conflict of interest to advise you to purchase insurance and then turn around and sell you the insurance product at the same time. Ask him/her to justify why you should carry an insurance product at such a young age.

There are two types of life insurance you may be told about, term life and permanent life. Term is just that, a life insurance policy in effect for a limited period of time, typically one, five, ten, or twenty years. Term is the cheapest form of life insurance because it rarely pays out and you (your family, actually) don't receive anything from this type of policy unless you die. This is the type of coverage that most employers offer you in their benefit packages. Permanent insurance can have many names in the industry, such as variable universal life (VUL), universal life (UL), and whole life (WL). These are just that, life insurance policies that last for the remainder of your life. These options cost considerably more than term and likewise carry a much higher commission (bonus) for the insurance agent who sells the product. This life insurance is going to pay out to your loved ones, assuming you continue to pay the insurance premiums until you die. The benefit to you, other than the peace of mind that your loved ones are covered, is that these policies can build up invested cash value that you can access after a period dictated by the insurance company (called a surrender period). These policies are right only for individuals who can properly fund the policy. Unless you have considerable discretionary income, have someone to protect, and have funded all your other retirement savings options, this probably isn't a good product for you.

In summary, get the one-times-salary coverage from your employer to cover final expenses (funeral and burial), and skip the rest unless you have a spouse and/or children.

Accidental Death and Dismemberment Insurance (AD&D)

AD&D insurance is not worth the minimal dollars that you'll pay to carry it. These policies pay out only in limited circumstances, and it's like gambling that you'll die of an accident rather than natural causes. I don't recommend spending time or money on this.

Workplace Retirement Plan / 401(k) or 403(b)

This section could be a book in and of itself and the prospect of retiring fifty years from now may not seem all that urgent. Where the urgency lies is establishing your employer-sponsored retirement plan if your employer is just itching to give you free money. I say "free money," but if you remember what I said about maximizing your work benefits as an extension of your wages, it isn't "free money" at all. In fact, it's part of your compensation, and you'd be a fool not to enroll and contribute up to the percentage necessary to receive the full employer matching-contribution.

Depending on your employer/industry, there may be a couple of options to choose from: a traditional 401(k), a Roth 401(k), a 403(b), or a Roth 403(b). Some of you may work for a smaller company that offers what is called a SIMPLE or SEP IRA. These are all fancy abbreviations/acronyms for retirement plans. Because the majority of you will fall under the 401(k) umbrella, I'll reference this plan going forward but the concepts are similar for the others.

The most common workplace retirement plan is the 401(k), and the difference between the traditional and Roth versions is how the money is taxed at the time you contribute to the plan and then again when you withdraw the money forty or fifty years from now, when you retire. The traditional 401(k) allows you to contribute a percentage of your paycheck into an account that can be invested in the stock market and grow tax deferred until you choose to withdraw the money in retirement. Now, if you remember the discussion of your paycheck deductions and how most of those came out before the tax was assessed, that is how the traditional 401(k) would work. It's as if the IRS doesn't even know you made that money, because they can't tax you on it yet. But rest assured they'll get their taxes when you use those dollars in retirement. The traditional 401(k) is ideal for someone who makes a lot of money and needs a tax break in the current year. The employee who contributes to this version of the 401(k) is betting that his/her tax rate will be lower when he/she retires, so it makes more sense to get the tax break now rather than later.

The Roth 401(k), on the other hand, is an after-tax contribution into a similar account that grows tax-free and allows for tax-free withdrawals as long as plan rules are followed. An employee who contributes to this version of the 401(k) is betting that his/her tax rate will be higher in the future and therefore is postponing the tax benefits until that time. Someone in your situation who is working his/her first job, in a low tax-bracket, and expects their income to increase considerably, should choose the Roth 401(k) and pay the taxes before contributing to this retirement account. This is the plan type and posttax deduction illustrated in our earlier example around understanding your paycheck.

How about that employer matching contribution that I alluded to before? This is the percentage that your employer will match against your contribution. Each employer is different, and each plan is different; just be thankful you're receiving a 401(k) match. As an example, my previous employer matched my contribution up to 5 percent. So, each paycheck, I contributed 5 percent and the company matched 5 percent, so I had the equivalent of 10 percent of my salary being contributed to my 401(k) account, and I put up only 5 percent.

Some of the matching-contribution scenarios aren't that straightforward, and it may not be a dollar-for-dollar match. For example, I've seen retirement plans that will match 50 percent of your contributions up to 3 percent. In this scenario, you would have to contribute 6 percent of your pay to receive a 3 percent match. The key takeaway is to contribute the amount necessary to maximize the employer-matching percentage.

Another point I would like to expand on is the tax-deferral arrangement of the employer matching contribution. No matter what plan type you choose, either traditional or Roth, the employer match will be tax deferred as it is in a traditional 401(k). So even if you are contributing after-tax dollars into a Roth 401(k) and building your tax-free retirement savings, the employer match will always be contributed as pretax dollars and grow tax deferred until you pull the money out in retirement, and you will pay taxes on that amount at that time. You will essentially have two separate 401(k) accounts, one that's tax deferred and one that is tax-free, although they will show up as one value on your quarterly statement. You don't have a choice on this, and frankly, it's good to have money in both buckets, because we don't know what the tax environment will be in fifty years.

One last thing: The 401(k) contributions are meant for retirement, and thus you should never touch those assets prior to turning fifty-nine and a half years of age. In the majority of scenarios, if you do pull these assets out (apart from a 401(k) loan), you will pay tax (at ordinary income tax rates) and a penalty of 10 percent on those distributions. Worse yet is the fact that you've just mortgaged your retirement for a frivolous reason. **Don't be tempted to do this**. I repeat: don't be tempted to do this! This book will get you prepared to meet your emergency needs to avoid this temptation at all costs.

If your employer does not offer a matching contribution, you may want to consider looking elsewhere once you gain work experience. Shop around for an employer with a salary and benefits that meet your needs.

If you end up leaving an employer and have the opportunity to roll the 401(k) into a new 401(k) or a traditional IRA, don't be tempted to pay the taxes and penalties and use the money to pay off debt or to use it as a down payment on a car or similar. This is a bad way to get behind on your retirement. Trust me; I've done it, and I kick myself every day.

Don't Wait to Start Saving in Your Retirement Plan

You may have just read the preceding paragraphs and still believe that you have plenty of time to save for retirement; you'll have fun now and worry about retirement later. Let's look at a few examples to illustrate my point of establishing your 401(k) savings immediately versus waiting five or even ten years. I've used a 3 percent increase in annual salary, a 3 percent 401(k) contribution, and a balanced portfolio with a modest, average 6.7 percent rate of return. I've run four scenarios, each retiring at 65 years of age:

- Starting the contributions immediately and receiving a 3 percent matching contribution

- Starting the contributions in five years and receiving a 3 percent matching contribution
- Starting the contributions in ten years and receiving a 3 percent matching contribution
- Starting immediately but receiving no employer matching contribution

Scenario 1: Starting the contributions immediately and receiving a 3 percent matching contribution

If you were to start your 3 percent contributions with a 3 percent matching contribution immediately, you would have accumulated $11,401 after five years, $28,910 after ten years, and $877,414 at retirement in 2065.

Scenario #2: Starting the contributions in five years and receiving a 3 percent matching contribution

If you were to start your 3 percent contributions with a 3 percent matching contribution after five years, you would have $0 after five years, $13,143 after ten years, and $692,061 at retirement in 2065.

Scenario #3: Starting the contributions in ten years and receiving a 3 percent matching contribution

If you were to start your 3 percent contributions with a 3 percent matching contribution after ten years, you would have $0 after five years, $0 after ten years, and $537,559 at retirement in 2065.

Scenario #4: Starting immediately but receiving no employer matching contribution

If you were to start your 3 percent contributions immediately with no employer match, you would have accumulated $5,700 after five years, $14,455 after ten years, and $438,707 at retirement in 2065.

	Strategy 1	Strategy 2	Strategy 3	Strategy 4
After 5 years	$ 11,401.00	$ -	$ -	$ 5,700.00
After 10 years	$ 28,910.00	$ 13,143.00	$ -	$ 14,455.00
At age 65	$ 877,414.00	$ 692,061.00	$ 537,559.00	$ 438,707.00

As you can see from the above numbers, the difference of waiting five or ten years can affect your ability to retire by age sixty-five. I included scenario 4 to illustrate just how important an employer matching contribution can be. Obviously, you probably wouldn't work for an employer for forty-seven years if you weren't getting a matching contribution, but I wanted to get the point across, so ditch that job (but not until you've secured another) and find better benefits.

My first goal is to get you to start your Roth 401(k) or Roth 403(b) and contribute up to the matching percentage. My next goal is to get you to increase those contributions by 1 percent every year until you reach the maximum contribution in the distant future. By raising your contribution by 1 percent per year for the first ten years (this wouldn't reach the maximum but is for illustration purposes), you could have $2.11 million by the time you retired at age 65 (assumptions of 3 percent match and 6.7 percent average rate of return). That 1 percent increase will capture not only your original annual income of $31,200 but the 3 percent annual increase in your salary as well. So, if you start with an income of $31,200 and in year 2 you receive a 3 percent merit increase (raise), you would be earning $32,136. A 1 percent increase to your Roth 401(k) would reduce your bi-weekly paycheck by $12.36. This is another example of **paying yourself first**. Set the increase at the beginning of the new year, and forget it; you won't miss it.

Investing Your Retirement Plan Contributions

Now, how to invest your contributions? The most important goal is establishing your retirement contributions up to the employer-matching percentage immediately. Next is investing those contributions. Initially, I wouldn't worry too much about how your dollars are invested, because again, you are looking at nearly forty to fifty years of savings and growth. Having said that, the calculations that I performed earlier using an investment portfolio with a growth rate of 6.7 percent can have wild swings with an adjusted rate of return of even 1 percent higher or lower. For now, look for something called a target fund, which your 401(k) may offer. A target fund will invest your dollars in a diversified portfolio with your specific timeframe in mind. For instance, if your presumed retirement date is 2065, you would look for the target fund 2065 and direct 100 percent of your contributions into that particular mutual fund. If you have a retirement year that is not a five-year multiple, look for the target fund closest to your projected retirement date. Eventually, you'll want to conduct a risk assessment to see how much volatility you can handle in the stock market. Just remember that the stock market is volatile and will fluctuate up and down on a daily basis, but we are concerned about long-term performance, so don't bother looking at your account other than monthly or even annually at this stage. Once you've performed a risk assessment and have a target allocation (percentage of stocks vs. bonds), you'll want to rebalance annually back to your original portfolio percentages. We'll go into more detail in the investments section, a bit later.

If a target fund is not available in your list of mutual fund choices, use a simple allocation that will diversify your investments. Diversification is the key to investing. History has taught us that different segments of the stock market will increase while others decrease in value, in any given year, and since we don't have a crystal ball or a program that can pick the winning formula, we need to have investments in each of the market segments (diversification). Again, this may be temporary, but it will allow your dollars to have the potential for growth while you determine your risk tolerance. Consider investing your 401(k) contributions with the following allocation, if the target fund is unavailable:

- 30 percent large cap (value or growth—if both are available, use 15 percent to each)
- 15 percent mid cap (doesn't matter whether growth or income)
- 15 percent international or global equity
- 10 percent small cap
- 10 percent emerging market (if not available, add 10% to international)
- 20 percent bond fund (long term)

If you're a more risk-averse investor, meaning you can't stomach wild fluctuations in the stock market, consider this allocation:

- 50 percent S&P 500 index fund or a large-cap growth/value fund (blend)
- 40 percent bond fund (long term, if available)
- 10 percent international or emerging markets

To reiterate, set up your retirement account through your employer, using the Roth option. Make this a priority immediately (after all this, if I find out you waited, I'll…), especially if your employer offers a matching contribution, and contribute the maximum needed to receive the full matching percentage. Use a target fund if available in your investment options or consider the allocation percentages above.

This concludes the employee-benefits portion of your guide. Don't stress out when making your selections. Use the guide, establish your health, dental, disability insurance to the maximum available, and life insurance to cover your final expenses (if single), and begin your retirement plan contributions immediately up to the matching percentage offered in a Roth 401(k) or 403(b).

Now that benefits are established, I want to impress upon you the evils of falling victim to debt and living above your means. Poor spending decisions now can affect your financial life for years, and in some cases, you may never recover.

Chapter 4

Credit Cards and Debt

I'M CONFLICTED WHEN I tell a young adult to build his/her credit score with the high probability of going into debt in the process. I'm putting a credit card in the hands of someone who isn't used to having access to this kind of purchasing power. Don't get me wrong: a credit card company will only provide access to a limited amount of credit, prior to the applicant displaying credit worthiness, but you could still be looking at a couple thousand dollars at a very high interest rate. Multiply that by five introductory cards with a $2,000 credit limit and you have an opportunity to get into a shitload of financial trouble. Once you've shown a pattern of making payments on time, the credit card companies will be quick to extend your credit limit even further, which is where you will have to show additional maturity and restraint beyond your years and use only credit you can pay off on a monthly basis. You should never extend yourself beyond your means. In other words, don't spend more than you earn. Responsible adults will typically find a credit card on which they can rack up frequent flier miles or cash back to use later for a free airline ticket or as cash on purchases. Some will pay their mortgages, car payments (if available), monthly utility bills, and so on, but pay off the balance from their checking accounts immediately. This isn't a terrible strategy, since you are getting something for using the card but you aren't paying the credit card company anything extra (unless paying an annual fee) for the ability to use the card. The credit card company is betting that you will either overextend yourself, lose your job or flat out forget to pay your bill so they can charge you interest. Companies can offer perks because the vast majority of their customers don't have the restraint to live within their means and pay the debt during the current billing cycle. To make some additional money off people who do pay their bills on time, the credit card companies may charge annual fees for the right to use their cards. These annual fees typically range from $35 to upwards of $200, depending on the perks offered.

Banks are in the business of making money off households carrying debt. They lend out dollars for credit card purchases, to buy a car, or the granddaddy of them all, to buy a house. They lend the money at rates that are clearly beneficial to the bank and less so for the borrower (you). For instance, if you take out a personal car loan through a bank, it is typically much higher than if you were to finance a car at a dealership. Someone in your situation would be offered a loan at about 8 percent, let's say. That same bank is offering to pay you a fraction of a percent to keep your money in a savings account at that bank, let's say 0.2 percent. So, if you have $1,000 invested in your savings account, over the course of a year, you will accrue $2 in interest. Over that same period, $1,000 borrowed from the same bank will cost you $80 (at 8% interest). That's revenue for the bank of $78. Now you see why Bank of America is worth a bazillion dollars. Of course, banks do provide a service that allows you to purchase something that wouldn't be attainable without the loan. A house worth a couple hundred thousand dollars can't be purchased with your small down payment of $10,000; you need someone with the resources to lend you the money to buy that house and then be paid back monthly for that service. We'll talk more about mortgages and home purchases in the "Where Do You Plan to Live?" section.

A mortgage on a home is what is referred to as good debt because you are getting a place to live that should actually appreciate in value, if history is any indication, and you are building equity in that asset that the bank helped you purchase. What I want to focus on in this section is bad debt, and for our purposes, I will limit the conversation to credit-card debt.

In American households with debt, on average, $15,355 of that debt is credit-card debt (NerdWallet, 2015). The average interest rate, as published by the Federal Reserve Bank, in 2015 was 13.66 percent. What that means is that if you don't pay the balance of the credit card before the billing cycle is over, you'll pay 1.14 percent per month (13.66 divided by twelve months) on the balance remaining on the card for that billing cycle. Let's say you are carrying a balance of $2,000 on a card. You will pay $22.80 in interest for that billing cycle. If you were to carry that balance for a full year, you would be looking at $273 in interest payments. You can understand where someone can get into trouble.

What makes matters worse is seeing friends with better jobs, making more income than you, flaunting better clothes, watches, purses, shoes—you get the picture. You want those things but can't afford those things. You've got that little plastic miracle worker in your pocket, and you will surely be getting a raise in the near future or a big tax refund you can use to pay off any credit-card balance at that time. You'll say, "Just this one time, I'll buy that purse or those new shoes on the card, and that will be it." You know what you just did? You just proved the credit card company right: you can't manage your impulses, desires, or money, and they've got another credit addict to make their shareholders happy. It's just another peddler feeding an addict. That may seem a bit harsh, but I've seen too many people that have nothing for retirement or for their children's education because of that one purchase they were going to make just that one time. You know what happened, they didn't get that raise or that tax refund they were expecting, or if they did, it went towards paying rent or the car payment instead, or for a new set of tires they weren't expecting to buy for another year. Don't be a slave to the credit industry. They're smarter than most and play the odds that life is going to happen and your best intentions won't be realized. You'll be paying their fat salaries for the next fifteen years as you try to get yourself out of that $15,355 in debt that you've accumulated on those "just this one time" purchases. **TAKE PRIDE IN BEING DEBT-FREE!**

Here's an example to illustrate my point further? And yes, this is intended to scare you.

If we use the average credit-card debt balance of $15,355 as an example, that household would be paying $175 per month in interest, or $2,100 per year, in interest payments. If they were to pay the minimum on this debt of $200 per month, it would take them fifteen years and three months to pay it off, and they would ultimately pay $21,240 in interest, in addition to the $15,355, for a total of $36,595. TAKE PRIDE IN BEING DEBT-FREE! The interest paid over that many years could have bought them a new car.

Building Your Credit

To be sure, you'll need to build your credit score to prove to future lenders that you are worthy of a lower interest rate. The bank wants that fuzzy feeling that if they lend you $200,000–$500,000 for a home mortgage, you won't default and they won't be stuck with a house that they have to maintain, pay for, and ultimately resell. Why your credit score matters to you is a lesson in simple math. Compare a mortgage of $250,000 for an individual (you) with a good credit score and one for a person with a crappy credit score. You could be talking about a minimum of 1 percent difference on the interest rate for that thirty-year mortgage. One percent doesn't seem like a lot, right? That's only one dollar out of every $100. But multiply that over thirty years, and $250,000 instead of $100, and you're looking at a difference of $53,466 over the life of that loan. Not to mention that your monthly mortgage payment would be $148 higher per month, which may not fit into your budget at that time. To strengthen your credit score, pay your credit card balance immediately after every purchase, and don't buy what you can't pay off the next day. It's really as simple as that. As soon as you set up the credit card, go to that company's site and establish an online payment, which will require you to enter your bank information. This process will take about ten minutes.

You might be asking yourself what a good credit score is and what you should be shooting for. Here's a guide to good and bad credit scores. You want to be in the good to excellent range (of course). You thought rankings would end once you got out of school? Think again.

Credit Score Range and Ranking (Experian 2017)

- 800+   Excellent
- 740–799   Very good
- 670–739   Good
- 580-669   Fair
- Below 580   Poor

How Credit Scores are Calculated (Experian 2017)

- 35%: Payment history (are you making your payments on time)
- 30%: Amounts owed on credit and debt (higher maintained debt, lower score)
- 15%: Length of credit history (this will improve over time)
- 10%: New credit (for you it will all be new)
- 10%: Types of credit used (cash advances vs. purchases)

Watch Out!

This is probably the most important part of this section: what to be cautious of when picking a credit card to build your credit score. Here is what to be cautious of when selecting your initial credit card and the caveats to remember when using said credit card:

- Look for a credit card with no annual fee.
- Look out for deceiving introductory interest rates. Don't be lazy here. Read the fine print, or call the company and ask about the interest rate breakdown and timeline. A bank may offer 0 percent (albeit probably not for a first-time card member) for the first six months and then inflate that interest rate to 15, 20, or 25 percent after that six-month period.
- If you don't make your monthly payment within sixty days, the bank can raise your introductory rate from 0 percent to as high as 29.99

percent. You wouldn't want to round this up to 30 percent, because that would be scary. Make the goddamn payment the day after the purchase, and don't spend what you can't afford. Sorry for the profanity, but this is important to instill early.

How to Get Out of Debt

As I stated earlier, credit cards should be required to carry skull and crossbones, a frowny-face or poop emoji on every card. Credit card debt has ended marriages, caused bankruptcies, and worst of all, led to suicides owing to the victims' despair and hopelessness about never being able to recover from this financial crisis. These are obviously extreme cases, and I'm not typically one to try to shock someone into learning a valuable lesson, but I want you to understand the potential magnitude of your spending habits while you're still in the formative stage of your life.

Now, let's say you thought you were smarter than the banks and didn't take my advice or were in debt prior to reading this book. How do you get out of the debt that you've accumulated?

First, cut up the goddamn card or cards that got you into trouble in the first place. You've proven (at least for the moment) that you can't be trusted with this temptation. Seriously, cut them up, or better yet, shred them so no one else can get their hands on them. Before you do anything, look at your bank account, and see what your cash-reserve balance is. Is there anything there? Typically not, if you've racked up debt. You've probably blown through your cash or weren't saving in the first place. If there is a balance in your checking or savings account, what are you waiting for? Use your cash to pay off the high-interest credit-card debt. Pay off the card with the highest interest rate first. If you have anything left, apply it to the card with the next-highest interest rate. If the credit cards carry a 0 percent interest rate, that's a different story, but for the most part, your cash savings are earning a fraction of a percent (twenty cents for every hundred dollars annually) compared to the debt that is potentially costing you exponentially more than that (twenty dollars per every hundred dollars owed annually).

If you don't have a cash reserve to pay off the debt, create a spreadsheet or take out a piece of paper, and write down the debt balance, interest rate, the dollar amount you are paying every month, and lastly, the required minimum payment for each card (see the example below). Put these in order from the highest interest rate to the lowest. Tally up the total amount you are currently paying on all the cards on a monthly basis. Now tally up the minimum-payment column for the month. Is there a difference between the two? I hope there is. Otherwise, you'll be paying these cards off for years. If there is a difference between the two columns, start paying the minimum on every card with the exception of the one at the top of the list, the one with the highest interest rate. Whatever extra payments you were paying above and beyond the minimums on the other cards should be applied to the highest-interest rate credit card. Trust me on this. You may feel better by paying a little extra on every one of your cards, but you are actually losing money on the deal. If you have a credit card with a balance of $5,000 that carries an interest rate of 20 percent and a credit card with a $5,000 balance that carries an interest rate of 10 percent, you're paying $83 per month in interest on the higher-rate card compared to $41.5 per month in interest on the 10 percent credit card. Pay down the card that is costing you the most every month. Make sense?

Once that card is paid off, you'll have freed up a large monthly payment that should be applied only toward the card that is second on your list. Don't use the freed-up money to buy something else. Use it to get out of debt, and then start paying yourself back by building your cash reserve.

Card	Balance	Interest Rate	Monthly Payment	Minimum Payment	Pay This
CITI Bank	$ 5,000	20%	$ 100	$ 75	$ 150
Bank of America	$ 1,000	10%	$ 75	$ 35	$ 35
Capitol One	$ 2,500	7%	$ 60	$ 50	$ 50
Total	$ 8,500	-	$ 235	$ 160	$ 235

In the example above, focus on the far-right column, which is titled "Pay This." I simply illustrate paying the minimum to the Bank of America and Capital One cards and add the additional payments from those cards to the Citibank monthly payment, with the highest rate at 20%.

Balance Transfers

To accelerate the credit card payoff, there is another strategy that could help you avoid interest payments altogether if you can find the right introductory-rate credit card. Banks will offer 0 percent introductory rates to lure transfer dollars to their card, but be careful of balance-transfer fees and the period for those introductory rates. Again, the bank offering this "great deal" may have hidden costs that will negate the strategy of transferring your high-interest balances to this new credit card. Make sure you can pay the balance off within that designated period, because the other caveat is the interest rate that follows that introductory period. Make sure that the rate doesn't balloon to a rate higher than your current interest rates once that period ends. The bank offering the new card is betting that your spending habits and penchant for debt balances will continue.

Summary

Stay out of credit-card debt, plain and simple. The concepts are pretty simple. Don't spend more than you can afford to pay back the next day. Live within your means. If you get into debt, pay off the card with the highest interest rate first and work your way down the list to the debt with the next-highest interest rate until all credit card balances are paid off. With the freed-up monthly payments, apply toward your cash reserve to avoid this mess in the future.

Keep in mind that your friends that you perceive to have everything, including the perfect life, are probably overextended and swimming in credit card debt themselves. Pay your shit off and be the envy of the neighborhood! On second thought, do it for yourself!!

Chapter 5

Investing

(Key words: diversification, dollar-cost averaging, compounding)

WITHOUT DEBT, YOU may have the means to save excess cash for a short- or long-term savings goal. This is after you've fully established your cash reserve. We've touched upon investing through the emergency-fund conversation and the employer-sponsored retirement plan but have only scratched the surface on this topic. This is where movies such as *Wall Street* (way before your time, but look it up on Netflix), *The Boiler Room*, *The Big Short*, *The Wolf of Wall Street*, and so on have glamourized the fat broker bonuses at the expense of the little guy. We'll keep it simple and avoid options, futures, derivatives, and short sales and instead talk about mutual funds and ETFs. With that, I'll give you a crash course on investing.

People devote their entire lives to the study of investing, and we're obviously not going into that amount of detail within this book, but I do want to share ideas for someone your age, in addition to some things to watch out for. Investing in this context is different from your cash reserve. This is all about longer-term investing in the stock market. The concepts talked about here will correlate with the investing that you'll be doing in your employer-sponsored retirement account (if available), but these investments will offer more flexibility and options owing to IRS withdrawal restrictions before the age of fifty-nine and a half on qualified retirement accounts.

Once your cash reserves are established, you may want to start saving for something more, such as a down payment on a home, starting your own business, buying a newer car, or even taking a dream vacation. The level of risk you are willing to take and the length of time you plan to have this sum of money invested should dictate the type of investment. If you are working toward a goal that will happen within the next three years, your appetite for stocks and the volatility that comes with the stock market may not be in your best interest. Leave the money in cash or something similar, such as certificates.

This way, you won't arrive at the goal date and be forced to push it back by a year because your investment hasn't grown as you anticipated, or worse yet, you've lost a considerable portion of your original investment. For goals five years out or longer, remember the word "diversification." Diversification is the key to long-term investing and should be the cornerstone of your workplace retirement account and longer-term strategies for major purchase goals. When diversifying, you are spreading your money across a wide spectrum of industries, company size (large, medium, small, micro), countries (domestic, international/global, emerging markets), and types (stocks, bonds, real estate, commodities, natural resources, etc.) of investments. In theory, the more you diversify, the less risk you take on, and the more soundly you'll sleep, knowing that your investment won't go to zero on the next trading day.

As indicated above, investments can range from individual stocks to bonds, real estate, precious metals (gold and silver), and oil and gas, or you can bundle these investments in the form of mutual funds and exchange-traded funds (ETFs). When you buy a single anything, whether a stock or a bond or any of the others, you run the risk of that company, industry, or sector experiencing volatility to the point that you can either make a lot of money or lose it all in the blink of an eye. I leave the stock-picking decisions to the experts who do this for a living. They are paid to research individual companies or sectors 24/7. I recommend diversifying that risk by using mutual funds or exchange-traded funds (ETFs), which, to reiterate, are collections of company stocks, bonds, precious metals, natural resources (oil and gas), real estate properties, and so on. If one of the companies in the mutual fund or ETF goes bankrupt (extreme I know), you have fifty (maybe less, but more than one) others to balance out the portfolio, so you may lose a little, but not everything. On the flip side, you won't double your money overnight either. You've got a long time to invest, so don't get greedy and go for the home run. As long as you invest wisely and give your money time to work for you, you won't have to buy into risky investments.

Beware

Beware of friends, family, Uber drivers or the guy next to you on the subway who claims to have the next big stock and brags about making a killing in the stock market. You only hear about the good ones. Trust me: this same guy/gal lost money on plenty of big losers but doesn't want you to know about those. This is the same person who goes to Vegas and wins $4,000 on a slot machine, then turns around and loses $5,000 on blackjack, but tells you only about the slot machine win. People want to look smart; no one broadcasts when they've made a colossal mistake.

Don't get caught up on message boards or blogs that tout individual stocks. You don't know these people, and most have a vested interest in getting you to buy that stock. They're already invested and want the share price to go up. It doesn't mean it's a good investment. They may have made a knee-jerk purchase, and the price has been plummeting ever since, so they need new investors to prop up the price enough to sell out of the position and lose a little less money.

Don't buy a company right after reading about a hot stock in *Money*, *Forbes*, or *Business Investor Daily* and think the stock is going to skyrocket. The smart money (investors) was already in the stock and will experience the price jump when the general public starts purchasing the stock after the article runs. Then the smart money will leave the stock, make their profits, and leave you holding the bag and waiting for the price to recover. Now, again, this may be a good investment, but it has to be something you are willing to hold for a long period of time (at least a year).

Don't day-trade stocks and think you're smarter than everyone else. You're not. Trust me: thousands have tried, and thousands have failed. You'll lose a ton of money on ticket (transaction) charges, and the gains that you do make will be eaten up by losses, short-term capital gain taxes, and wash sales (selling, then buying same stock within 30 days, which negates the loss). Don't do this.

In Summary:

- Don't buy individual stocks; diversify through ETFs or mutual funds and invest for the longer term.
- Don't listen to stock tips from friends or family who claim to be "killing it."
- Don't buy stocks that you read about and think you'll make a killing short-term.
- Don't day-trade stocks.

The moral of the story is to diversify risk by using mutual funds and ETFs. I always want clients to understand what they are getting into, the methodology, and the cost of that investment. Here is a brief synopsis:

Mutual Funds

Mutual funds were created to make investing easier and less risky for the common investor. A mutual fund is a pool of money that individual investors collectively use to purchase stock in many companies to satisfy a common goal and diversify risk. That goal may be to invest in the best large-cap growth companies in the United States, such as Apple, Google, and Amazon (for instance). That is just one of many possibilities. Others include small cap, mid cap, tech, biotech, natural resources, and so on. The abbreviation "cap" stands for capitalization, and this represents the corporate valuation of the companies in that segment—in other words, what the company is worth, typically in billions of dollars.

If you choose to purchase mutual funds, be aware that there are different cost structures to these investments. You have load and no-load mutual fund options. Loaded funds have different share classes—A, B, and C. In the case of an A-share, you are required to pay an up-front fee (called a load), which can range from 2 percent to as much as 6 percent of the investment amount, to get into this particular fund. B-shares (these are being phased out) require you to pay a percentage of the overall value at the time you leave the investment, which is similar to an A-share percentage but on the back end. On top of that, the A and B share classes will require you to pay an annual maintenance/management fee, in the neighborhood of 1 percent. Lastly, C-shares do not charge anything on the front or back end but charge a higher yearly management fee as a percentage of the fund value, sometimes close to 2 percent. You can imagine this can get pretty costly if you are paying 5 percent on a $1,000 purchase (a cost of $50) and internal fees of 1 percent ($10) per year per $1,000 invested. This will cut into your profit.

At this stage of your life, I recommend working directly with one of the no-load fund companies, such as Vanguard or T. Rowe Price, and holding your funds there. These funds charge a relatively low transaction fee to process the trade and typically have lower yearly maintenance/management fees. Rest assured you will pay something for your investment, but it is on the order of 0.2–1.0 percent per year to the fund manager. He/she needs to earn a living and is the person determining what to buy and sell inside your mutual fund, and I can live with that. With no-load funds, you're saving on the investment purchase and sale. Whether the investment amount is $1,000 or $10,000, the transaction fee should be the same low-dollar amount rather than a percentage of the invested dollars. On a $10,000 purchase of a no-load fund, you may pay a $15 transaction fee rather than a $500 fee on an A-share (loaded fund) purchase. Make sense?

Make sure you are looking at the internal annual management costs on your investments as well, to find the investment option that provides the highest total return. A half-percent difference in management fees over your lifetime can mean tens of thousands of dollars. When in doubt, ask as many questions as you need to of the establishment you are working with, because the industry is notorious for hiding fees to keep you in the dark about the true cost.

Exchange-Traded Funds

Exchange-traded funds (ETFs) were intended to capture the essence and diversification of mutual funds but have the added benefit of easy trading and lower overall expenses. ETFs are the younger brother, or actually the great-grandson, of the mutual fund. Mutual funds have been around since the 1890s, whereas ETFs have a relatively short history, dating back to 1993 (Investopedia). Similar to mutual funds, ETFs allow you to buy into a fund that invests in many companies, thus diversifying your dollars rather than putting all your eggs in one basket. ETFs are easy to track through the course of the day using any stock-quote engine, such as Yahoo Finance, StockQuote. com, or CNN Money.

You'll have to purchase ETFs through a brokerage house rather than at an individual fund company. Brokerage houses, such as Schwab, TD Ameritrade, Scottrade, and E-Trade, are good options for cost-effective investing. Transaction costs are generally between five and thirteen dollars per trade. That price will be the same to buy into and sell out of the ETF and is not based on a percentage of value (one flat fee in and out).

Similar to mutual funds, you can put together a collection of ETF sectors or market capitalizations to diversify your portfolio. I would recommend sticking with index ETFs that give you exposure to large, mid, and small caps, emerging markets, international stocks, and domestic and global bonds. This provides diversification over industries, sectors, and countries to capture opportunity and spread risk. To further dilute risk of timing purchases in the stock market, I want to introduce you to a concept called dollar-cost averaging and revisit our old friend compounding.

Dollar-Cost Averaging

The golden rule of investing is buy low and sell high. Unfortunately, many investors have gone crazy trying to decide what is low and what is high. No one has a crystal ball to see when a terrorist attack may affect the stock market or to know that a CEO has been embezzling millions of dollars, sending the company share price into a tailspin as he's walked to jail, streaming live on CNN. The smallest domestic or global disruption can cause the next stock market rally or collapse. Whether you're investing in mutual funds or ETFs, I recommend saving the same dollar amount on a monthly or biweekly (every pay period) basis, systematically. This strategy is known as dollar-cost averaging. By doing so, you are not trying to time the stock market, and in theory, over time, you will level out by buying at low and high points in the stock market cycle. You will capitalize on dips (buying cheap shares), while at other times, unfortunately, buying at a high point only to experience a bear market (remember bear means bad and bull means good). Always look at the bright side; while you're in that bear market for two years, you're gobbling up cheap shares because you are dollar-cost averaging during the prolonged dip. If history is any indication of future events, the market always corrects and always recovers. Just be patient, and if you can't be patient, stay in cash (in a savings account).

Compounding

Do you remember the first couple of pages, when I asked you what you'd choose, $1 million immediately or one penny doubled each day for a month? That was a lesson in compounding. If you invest hard-earned dollars, you should reasonably expect to make a return on that investment, whether interest on savings or stock-price appreciation. In theory, as you invest and earn a percentage per month on that investment, you are increasing your wealth. In addition, you are adding more savings to the pot each month through dollar-cost averaging, which increases your wealth even more. Now those new dollars, in addition to the original investment and the earnings on that investment, are earning a return monthly. Before you know it, this little ball of money is gaining momentum and size as it rolls down the proverbial hill called life. Time is your best friend when it comes to compounding. Every little bit of money that you can save over the course of your life should grow over time. How quickly it grows depends on many factors, such as your ability to stomach stock market volatility, but again, you can limit the anxiety through proper diversification. Are you getting sick of that word yet? I feel like I've typed it a thousand times, but that's good. If you're sick of hearing about it, then I've done my job, and hopefully its sticking with you.

Let's do a little calculation to illustrate the concept of compounding to get you excited about investing. Let's say you start with $100 in savings at the first of the year and establish a systematic monthly savings of $100 to add to that account. Let's also assume you are able to get a 5 percent rate of return on those invested dollars over that year. We'll break that 5 percent up into a monthly return of 0.42 percent (0.05 / 12 = 0.0042, or 0.42 percent). Here's how that first year would shake out:

- You save an initial $100 on January 1, $100 × 1.0042 = $100.42 at the end of January
- You save an additional $100 on February 1, $200.42 × 1.0042 = $201.26
- You save and additional $100 on March 1, $301.26 × 1.0042 = $302.52

- You save $100 on April 1, $402.52 × 1.0042 = $404.22
- Save $100 on May 1, $504.22 × 1.0042 = $506.33
- Save $100 on June 1, $606.33 × 1.0042 = $608.88
- Save $100 on July 1, $708.88 × 1.0042 = $711.86
- Save $100 on August 1, $811.86 × 1.0042 = $815.27
- Save $100 on September 1, $915.27 × 1.0042 = $919.11
- Save $100 on October 1, $1,019.11 × 1.0042 = $1023.39
- Save $100 on November 1, $1,123.39 × 1.0042 = $1,128.11
- Save $100 on December 1, $1,228.11 × 1.0042 = $1,233.27

I could go on and on, but I'm sure most of you are bored silly right now. The point is you've gained $33.27 over the course of the year, and now, hopefully, you've gotten a salary or wage increase or have paid off some debt and can increase the monthly savings to $200 or $300 per month to accelerate this snowball even quicker. You'll be in that house, new car, or on that beach in no time.

Oh, one last thing: That $33.27 that you earned over that year? That's not all yours. The government is going to expect a portion. Sorry to burst your bubble. Next up, **TAXES. Yay!!!!!!!!**

Chapter 6

Filing Your First Tax Return

THIS IS PROBABLY my least favorite topic to write about and potentially the least favorite for you to read about. Unfortunately, this is one of those times in life when you have to sit down, suck it up, and take care of business once a year.

You will be required to file a federal and state tax return for the state in which you live, unless you live in a state that does not have a state income tax. If you are in Alaska, Florida, Nevada, South Dakota, Texas, Washington, or Wyoming, you won't have to file a state tax return. If you live in New Hampshire or Tennessee, you don't have to file a return if you don't have interest or dividend income.

Now, if you work in a different state from where you live, things get a bit trickier. Since this situation is fairly rare for someone right out of high school, I'll consider it beyond the scope of this book. If you live in one state and work in another, I would recommend discussing your tax situation with a professional at H&R Block or similar for the first year to know how to file for the next year on your own.

Some Quick Facts about Filing Your First Tax Return (as of this writing, 2018 numbers are not published)

- Tax returns for income earned in 2018 need to be filed by April 15, 2019.
- For 2017, any nondependent (can't be claimed by his/her parents on their tax return) individual with W-2 income greater than $10,400, unearned income of $1,050, or self-employment income in excess of $400 is required to file a return for the previous year. Note: Meeting anyone of these numbers will require a tax return to be filed.
- For 2017, if you can still be claimed on your parents' tax return (you are a dependent), you will have different filing requirements. If you

are still considered a dependent of your parents, then you will have to file a tax return if you made W-2 income greater than $6,350, unearned income of $1,050, or self-employment income of $400 or more. Again, meeting anyone of these numbers will require a tax return to be filed.

- If you don't know, there is no harm in filing the return (as long as it's free). You may find that you are getting money back anyway.
- Tax returns can be filed through tax software such as TurboTax, H&R Block's website, or, for the cost of a stamp, by paper copy through regular postal mail (Form 1040EZ can be downloaded from IRS.gov).
  - There is a great resource offered on IRS.gov called Free File that will ask you six easy questions and tell you which tax software will file a federal and state tax return for free. These options are available only for individuals with income under $62,000. Individuals with income over $62,000 will pay a fee to file the returns. I recommend the **IRS.gov/FreeFile** website to find the software for you.

What You'll Need

- Time. Anywhere from thirty minutes to an hour, depending on how long it takes you to navigate the tax software.
- W-2 from your employer. This form is a record of your income, all taxes withheld, and pretax deductions that will be mailed to you (some available online through your employer) in January for the previous year's employment. If you have multiple salaried or hourly jobs, you'll receive a W-2 for each.
- Form 1099 that will be sent to you from your bank or brokerage company (for interest/investment income).
- And most importantly, a commitment to excellence! Just kidding, I made this one up. Sounds like a pep talk you may have gotten from your high school gym teacher. You don't have to be excellent. Trust me: just file the return.

Filing the Return

I recommend using the free filing software that I provided the link to above, but if you choose to do the paper copy, first and foremost, I'll warn you that your eyes will probably start to bleed if you try to read everything within the form and/or the form's instructions. **Don't do it.** Just do the checklist on page 6 of the instructions to determine whether you can file the 1040EZ form and then whether you qualify for the earned income credit (page 16 of the instructions). The earned income credit is available only to individuals with W-2 income less than $15,000 (single filer, at the time of this writing).

Next step, fill out the return and determine whether you owe or expect a refund. It will literally take you minutes, especially if you are using the software. Go ahead. I'll wait.

Congratulations, chances are you got a refund for the year. Go buy a gift, or go out for dinner for less than forty dollars, and put the remainder into your savings account to boost your cash reserve. If your return was $500 or more, I suggest that you go onto your work website or talk to your human resources rep and look for or ask about the W-4 filing (a tax form you filled out when you started with your employer) and adjust your withholdings. The number of withholdings determines how much you get in your paycheck. Use the IRS withholdings calculator to determine what is appropriate (www.irs. gov/individuals/irs-withholding-calculator). This will allow you to get more money back during the course of the year rather than as one big lump sum at the end of the year. This will let you increase the dollar-cost-averaging sum you're saving per paycheck and accelerate that compounding effect. Again, I would only do this if your refund is $500 or more.

As we learned while breaking down your paystub, you will need to file a state tax return unless you live in Alaska, Florida, Nevada, South Dakota, Texas, Washington, or Wyoming (or New Hampshire and Tennessee if you don't have interest or dividend income). For all you poor saps who live in the other forty-one states, you will be using other boxes from your W-2 (labeled "State Income/Tax"). If you are using a tax-filing software through IRS.gov/FreeFile, you will be prompted to choose your state. Just follow the prompts, answer the questions, and you'll be done in minutes. Most software will remember entries from the federal return so you don't have to reenter the data/numbers.

See, that wasn't so bad, was it? Boring as hell for sure, but not hard when you just use the software.

I'm assuming you've heard the phrase, "The only two certainties in life are death and taxes." Well, you've just experienced the latter. Let's make sure you don't experience the former for at least seventy more years, because you've got some living to do. Now let's cover some of those financial decisions you'll be making now that you're earning some CHEDDA!

Chapter 7

Transportation
(What Are You Going to Drive?)

NOW, HOW ARE you going to get to and from work, go to the grocery store, visit friends, or travel across the United States on a well-deserved vacation?

You've got multiple options for postgraduate transportation:

- Buy a new car
- Lease a new car
- Buy a used car
- Continue driving your parents' piece of crap

This is one of the biggest financial mistakes that individuals across all age groups make, especially those with limited cash flow. Buying a new car is a luxury that most of you graduating from high school cannot afford. The car companies are making it easier and easier for you to make a horrible decision by offering low interest rates and cash back for those who qualify (chances are you won't qualify with your limited to no credit history). This goes for the option to lease these "fantastic" vehicles as well. You can typically lower the monthly and down payments by leasing a vehicle, since the loan value is calculated using the expected sale price at the end of your three-year lease, not the full purchase price as if you were buying the car outright. Credit score requirements are typically higher with leases than with a new-car purchase as well.

We'll look at all the options bulleted above from a financial standpoint and discuss the ramifications of poor financial decisions in this space. This decision has a tendency to repeat itself throughout adulthood and can postpone other, presumably more important goals down the line. Take impulse out of your decision!

How Do You Get Around Now?

Let's start with how you get around currently in high school. Did your parents give you a car, did you hitch a ride with friends, or did you just stay home because you didn't have a way to get around? If you have a car currently, how does it make you feel to be seen in it? How much does that car cost on a monthly basis? Could you put the temptation of buying a new car aside long enough to save for a used car or, better yet, save money in your cash reserve and provide the protection (insurance) that I talked about earlier in the book? We'll crunch some numbers, and I'll show you a breakdown of the financial effects of the options above. Keep in mind that this decision, like every other decision that you make going forward, will have impacts on your financial present and future. Remember to **TAKE PRIDE IN BEING DEBT-FREE.**

Buying a New Car

Buying a new car has become a rite of passage, marking the transition from childhood to adulthood. In most cases, this is a terrible decision for graduates and one of the worst investments for someone in your particular situation. You'll look cool, don't get me wrong, but you'll also be mortgaging your future for the moment while you try to keep up with the rest of your friends making similar bad decisions. Let's weigh the advantages and disadvantages of the new-car purchase.

Advantages of Buying New

- Look cool
- Comfortable ride
- Look cool (this is duplicated for effect)
- Reliability
- Warranty if the car breaks down
- Limited to no maintenance
- Look cool (getting the point?)
- That new-car smell
- And last but not least, look cool (I'm bludgeoning you with this)

Disadvantages (for Most Recent Grads)

- You'll usually have a down payment of 10–20 percent of the purchase price ($3,000 to $6,000 on a $30,000 car/truck). This and the interest rate will determine monthly payments.

- It's a depreciating investment: you'll lose 10 percent as soon as you leave the lot and continue losing up to 55 percent by the end of year 3.
- You'll have monthly payments. For that same $30,000 car with $6,000 paid at signing, you'll pay $385 per month for six years (calculated with a 4.9 percent interest rate).
- You may not be able to afford to have fun with your friends, because of the monthly payment.
- You'll have higher monthly insurance costs due to having to carry full coverage.
- You may have to live in your car or with your parents because you won't be able to afford rent.
- You won't have any money to put toward your cash reserve.
- You are no longer debt-free, and the likelihood goes up that you'll begin to accumulate more debt to fund the lifestyle that you want because you are now cash poor with the car payment each month.

What if you could refrain from drooling over the TV and Internet ads that show the SUV driving over boulders and tree stumps while you sip your Starbuck's cappuccino? Let's be honest: for most of you, the closest you'll come to off-roading is driving over a median or curb while messing around with your friends.

Unless you've established your cash reserve, secured health and disability insurance, set up your retirement contributions, and saved a down payment on a new home (if that is a goal) and you have the additional means to cover your own insurance and the cash flow to cover a monthly car payment, generally in excess of $250 ($385 per month in the example above), this is a bad decision. To reiterate, new vehicles don't hold their resale value. On average, a new car depreciates 10 percent the moment you drive off the lot. That, in simple math, means that if you pay $30,000 for a car and drive it a hundred feet out of the dealership, you could resell it for $27,000. By the end of the first year, the car could be sold for $24,300, an additional 10 percent loss. If you lost 20 percent on an investment in the stock market, you'd probably sell it for a loss, lick your wounds, and move on, but a new car just keeps on giving, and by "giving," I mean kicking your financial ass and losing you money.

Take it from a guy who had two new-car payments after graduating from college back in the '90s, one for me and one for my fiancée. That was about $650 per month in car payments. I could have set aside those dollars every month for a down payment on a house, an investment that does actually appreciate and can potentially turn into an income producer later in life.

Let's look at what those monthly payments could look like if they were saved over the duration of the loan-repayment period of six years. We'll assume that the same down payment will be available for your existing car's maintenance, new tires, replacing tire bearings, new rotors, new brakes, a few headlights and taillights, and so on and therefore not considered for this savings exercise. We'll invest the $385 per month to save over those same seventy-two months. Simple addition with no return on that investment equates to $27,720. Now if you apply a 5 percent rate of return on those monthly savings over the same period, you'll have accumulated $31,461 (investment income taxed annually). That's a 20 percent down payment on a $157,000 house.

It really comes down to your priorities in life. I'll leave you with a guarantee. You won't mind paying the monthly payments for the first year, because of the new-car exhilaration (oh, the smell too), but once the honeymoon phase wears off, you'll begin to dread the $385 per month for the remaining five years. Trust me on this.

Leasing a New Car

Years ago, a board of directors got together in a big stuffy boardroom and listened to a pitch from a scrawny finance guy with wire-rimmed glasses and low self-esteem. Let's call this guy Ernie. Ernie talked about letting consumers drive a new car for a period of time, let's say three years, similar to renting a car from Avis or Hertz for a monthly fee, rather than a daily rate. Now the cards had to be stacked in the auto company's favor, so there had to be interest charged on the rental, and there had to be penalties if the consumer drove the vehicle too much; otherwise, the company would lose money. Once the smoke cleared, Ernie stood up to a round of applause and a pat on the back. He received a $500 bonus at the end of the year, and the company made millions. The new-car lease was born. *I completely made this up for dramatization sake, but probably not far from the truth.*

For qualified consumers, the leasing option provides an opportunity to drive a new car for three years (typically) while keeping the down payment and monthly payments more reasonable. Many times, the financing (interest rate) is more favorable as well, but to qualify, you have to have an established credit history and generally a good credit score (or cosigner). Here are some things to consider:

Advantages (*Compared to Equivalent New-Car Purchase*)

- Look cool
- Lower monthly payments
- Lower down payment (due at signing)

- Potentially lower interest rates (for those who qualify)
- Chance to sample a new car every three years
- Reliable and warrantied

Disadvantages

- You are paying a signing fee (down payment) and monthly payments but not building equity or essentially owning anything (you're renting this car for three years).
- You are locked into the lease for typically three years or longer.
- After three years, you have nothing to show for the payments; you do not own the car, and you're back where you were three years ago.
- You have limits on the amount you can drive the car, usually ten to twelve thousand miles per year.
  - You are typically penalized/charged fifteen cents per mile over the limit. That's $150 per one thousand miles over the limit.
- You have higher monthly insurance costs due to having to carry full coverage.

As you can see, this isn't a preferred option, for a number of reasons. You're renting a car for three years, wasting money in the process, and postponing a more definitive decision until your lease is up. In addition, you have the potential for penalties if you don't ration miles. **Skip the lease.**

Buying a Used Car

So how about buying used? That's got to be the preferred option, right? Under the right circumstances, it very well could be, but it comes with its own set of perils. How much do you trust a used-car salesman? Have you ever heard this line, "He's as shady as a used-car salesman"? As in any other profession, the salesman has to make a profit, and the less he/she can purchase a car for and dress it up and resell it, the larger the profit margin. Many of the used cars at dealerships come from trade-ins. The trade-in seems like a great deal when someone is shopping for a new car, because the trade-in is convenient and timely. It's an impulse decision allowing someone to get into that new car he/she so desperately needs (sarcasm) immediately.

The markup on a used-car trade-in and subsequent resale is as high as 50 percent to leave room for negotiation. Let's look at the advantages and disadvantages:

Advantages

- Typically, a lower cost than buying new
- Lower monthly payments or, if done right, paid in full
- Large part of initial depreciation is valued into the car's purchase price
- Costs less to insure, on average
- Can be sold or traded in at any time

Disadvantages

- You're buying a car from someone you don't know, and it could be a piece of junk.
- The car may not be under warranty, so you are buying it at your own risk.
- If the car is out of warranty, you will have to cover all costs of repairs/breakdowns.
- If you have to finance a portion of the car purchase price, you will typically have a higher interest rate through a private lender (if the dealership doesn't offer financing).

The key to buying used is making sure that if you are not an auto mechanic yourself, you have someone with experience inspect the car before buying it. The last thing you want to do is pay several thousands of your hard-earned dollars for a piece of crap that costs additional thousands to make drivable. This is truly a buyer-beware transaction. Now, if you buy from a dealership, you'll pay an additional markup, but you can potentially get a warranty for a limited period, and the dealership's reputation is on the line, especially in this day and age of internet ratings and reviews. You can do a lot of damage to the reputation of a dealership if you get screwed, and they know it.

My recommendation: Drive your beat-up jalopy for as long as you can and make a joke out of it, if you must. As a last resort, buy a used car that's at least three years old and depreciated by the estimated 55%. Take someone with you who knows how to inspect the car, and it doesn't hurt to have someone with negotiating skills to flat out ask the dealer about his markup and the car's history. Ask about any remaining warranties on the car. Once you've made the purchase you'll want to make sure that you increase your cash reserve for the inevitable used-car breakdown, but in the long run, you're talking about hundreds of dollars to potentially a few thousand, compared to six years of $385 payments per month ($27,720).

Remember:

- Look for a used car that is two to three years old or older.

- Try to get a car with a remaining warranty (some dealerships will give you a limited warranty if the factory warranty has expired).
- Keep your payments as small as possible. Pay cash if possible, but don't use up your cash reserve.
- If you are not buying from a dealership, make sure you have the car inspected by a trusted mechanic, friend, or family member who is qualified.

Now that you've identified a car, you haven't forgotten about insuring it, have you? Remember the days when you just put gas in your car and your parents took care of the rest? Welcome to adulthood. Before you get that car, get a quote through your parents' insurance agent, or through Progressive or Geico. com. Make sure you can afford your monthly car payment and the associated insurance premium. The following quotes are eye-opening and in some cases, can be higher than the actual monthly car payment. If you can't afford both, it's back to the drawing board or start walking.

Chapter 8

Buying Car Insurance

As FAR AS I'm concerned, car insurance can be compared to the tax section. Nobody likes to think about buying it, and I hate writing about it, but we have to discuss it nonetheless. If you are going to own a car, it's a necessity of life. Most states require some level of insurance to protect the other vehicle, the occupants of that vehicle, and the occupants in your vehicle if you happen to be the cause of an accident. The line items can be pretty confusing, and frankly, not knowing which are necessary or unnecessary can put a strain on your budget in the long run. In this section we'll discuss what's important, what's nice to have, and lastly, what's not that important, especially with an older used car.

Knowing what factors play into the cost of insurance premiums is a must *before* you purchase a new or used vehicle (Allstate, 2016 for much of the following).

- Type of car (expensive cars are costly to fix, and this will be reflected in the premium)
- New cars with loans and leased vehicles will require full coverage
- Driving record (insurers will charge more for driving infractions)
- Where you live and park your car (bad neighborhood, higher premium)
- Distance of commute (longer drive, higher chance of accident, higher premium)
- Gender and age (historical data plays into this bias)
- Deductibles and limits
  - Similar to health insurance, you will be responsible for the deductible before the insurer pays anything (higher deductible, lower monthly premium)
- Coverage line items (more coverage, more cost)

You'll still want to work with a trusted insurance professional but knowing the terminology and having an idea of the coverage you need prior to the consultation will help your confidence immensely. Your parents' insurer may be a good place to start, he or she will be less likely to screw you over if they risk losing your parents' business. Here are the common coverage terms you'll run across when selecting car insurance:

Liability Coverage

In most states, liability coverage is mandatory. There are two parts, bodily injury and property damage.

- *Bodily injury liability* covers injuries to your passengers and the driver and passengers of the other vehicle if you are at fault in an auto accident.
- *Property damage liability* covers damage to someone else's property if you are at fault in an auto accident. Usually this means damage to someone else's car, but it can also include damage to other types of property (fence, house, mailbox, etc.).

Medical Coverage: Protects You and Your Passengers

The type of medical coverage, medical expense or personal injury protection, depends on the state in which you live.

- *Medical expense* pays for medical care provided to you and your passengers as a result of a covered car accident, regardless of which driver is at fault.
- *Personal injury protection* helps reimburse you and your passengers for lost income, child care expenses, medical expenses, and other expenses if you are hurt in a covered accident, regardless of which driver is at fault. Examples include ambulance fees, hospital expenses, physician services, and funeral expenses.

Uninsured/Underinsured Motorist

Uninsured motorist coverage protects you if you are injured in an accident and the other driver is uninsured. It also protects you if you are the victim of a hit-and-run or are struck by a vehicle as a pedestrian.

Even if the other driver does have insurance, he/she may cause more damage than his/her insurance covers. In this case, underinsured motorist protection may help pay the balance.

Collision Coverage

This covers accidental damage caused by collision or rollover, regardless of who is at fault. Collision coverage is subject to a deductible amount. The higher the deductible, the lower the premium. If there is a collision claim on your policy, the deductible is the amount you will be required to pay before your insurance takes over to cover the balance.

Examples include collision with other vehicles, collision with stationary objects, rollover, and collision while parked.

Comprehensive Coverage

This covers damage or loss to your vehicle caused by things other than a collision or rollover. Comprehensive coverage is subject to a deductible also. Many comprehensive claims are weather or nature related. For those of you country bumpkins out there, this is running into a deer during the rut, which my family did twice in one year while I was growing up.

Examples include glass breakage, collision with animals, hail, wind, flood, vandalism, theft, fire, and falling objects.

This is a lot of terminology, and frankly, the lines between each may seem blurry. I wish you could get one package called the "don't screw me over, please" insurance package, but I haven't found that bundle yet. The thing to remember is what you are insuring. You will always want to be able to cover the passengers of both vehicles if you are at fault. You also want to be able to cover the property of the other individual if you are at fault (car or other property). Every state but New Hampshire will require liability insurance at a minimum. The minimum requirements for each state can be found on the following Nerd Wallet web page: https://www.nerdwallet.com/blog/insurance/car-insurance.

After that, think about what your car is worth to you. If this is an old clunker you are using while you save dollars for your next gently used car, then it may not make sense to purchase the other lines of insurance. I have a 2003 Toyota Corolla as a second car, and we maintain only liability insurance and underinsured/uninsured motorist on that car. If you are driving a new car and are insuring that (albeit depreciating) investment, you will want to make sure you can cover the replacement cost in the event of an accident. If you have a loan on a new vehicle or are leasing a new car, you won't have an option; the lease agreement or purchase agreement will dictate full coverage. Make sure you factor the cost of insurance into your budget before you buy the car, unless you want to eat ramen noodles and peanut butter sandwiches while you live with your parents the rest of your life.

I entered the information for an 18-year-old man in the Minneapolis area, into the Geico online calculator. I've provided all the line items so you can get a sense of the cost of each. This is based on a ten-year-old Toyota Camry, which is one of the most commonly owned cars. Keep in mind that these rates will vary by insurance company, driving record, and state. Notice the driver has no infractions/demerits on his record.

- 2008 Toyota CAMRY LE (Demerit Points: 0)
- Discounts Applied:
  - Air Bag
  - Seat Belt
- Deductible: $250
- Bodily Injury Liability: **$237.60**
  - $250,000 Per Person (each person in car is covered to this amount)
  - $500,000 Per Occurrence (total coverage per accident)
  - Property Damage Liability $100,000 Per Occurrence: **$252.40**
- Personal Injury Protection $40,000 Per Person: **$251.80**
- Comprehensive with $250 Deductible: **$75.70**
- Collision with $250 Deductible: **$379.60**
- Uninsured Motorist: **$10**
  - $250,000 Per Person
  - $500,000 Per Occurrence
- Underinsured Motorist: **$17.80**
  - $250,000 Per Person
  - $500,000 Per Occurrence
- Emergency Road Service: **$15.30**
- Rental Reimbursement: **$18.60**
- **Total Premium: $1,258.80 (per 6 months)**

As you can see, this is nearly as much as a monthly car payment ($210 per month) for a ten-year-old car. I may suggest this coverage instead due to the age and replacement cost of the car:

- 2008 Toyota CAMRY LE (Demerit Points: 0)
- Discounts Applied:
  - Air Bag
  - Seat Belt
- Deductible: $250
- Bodily Injury Liability: **$237.60**
  - $250,000 Per Person (each person in car is covered to this amount)

- □ $500,000 Per Occurrence (total coverage per accident)
- □ Property Damage Liability $100,000 Per Occurrence: **$252.40**
- Personal Injury Protection $40,000 Per Person: **$251.80**
- Comprehensive with $250 Deductible: **$0 (declined)**
- Collision with $250 Deductible: **$0 (declined)**
- Uninsured Motorist: **$10**
  - □ $250,000 Per Person
  - □ $500,000 Per Occurrence
- Underinsured Motorist: **$17.80**
  - □ $250,000 Per Person
  - □ $500,000 Per Occurrence
- Emergency Road Service: **$0 – get AAA (provides broader coverage)**
- Rental Reimbursement: **$0 (bum rides until you find a different car)**
- **Total Premium: $769.60 (per 6 months)**

With the revised coverage, you're looking at $128.26 per month, which is a bit more budget friendly. You may be able to get further discounts by being a good student (don't lie though) and increasing your deductible to $1,000. Again, make sure you've got your cash reserve established to cover the increased deductible. This is the bare bones policy that primarily covers liability, medical and the other driver if he or she is uninsured or underinsured.

In addition, this is one of many moments when it pays to have a good relationship with your parents. If they can keep you on their insurance plan, they are presumably getting discounts through their insurer for having multiple lines, such as homeowner's insurance, boat, multiple cars, and so on, and the costs will be considerably lower. So, kiss up to Mom and Dad if you have the opportunity. You can still pitch in your portion, but the monthly premiums should be considerably less.

Also, once you reach age twenty-five, apparently your ability to drive without an accident miraculously improves overnight. Your insurance premiums will generally decrease as long as your record is clean.

What to Do If You Are in a Car Accident

If you are in an accident, call the police immediately, then make sure you're all right and make sure you're not in harm's way before you get out of the car. Next, apply your hazard lights to ensure your vehicle can be seen by oncoming traffic. If it is safe to do so, exit the vehicle and never claim fault for anything. Use your phone to take pictures of any potential damage to each of the cars (again making sure not to put yourself in harm's way). Exchange driver's license and insurance-card information, and wait for the police to arrive. If the other driver is not willing to wait for the police, try to exchange information, especially name, phone number, license plate number and insurance-card information, before he/she leaves the scene. If you can, take a picture of his/her insurance card, license plate number, and any damage to his/her car that could be a result of the accident.

With this information, you'll have what you need to file an accident report and provide the details needed to your insurance agent or claims representative. Call your insurance agent as soon as you can to report the incident and find out what the next steps are. If you are not in a small town where everyone knows one another, you'll probably have a separate phone number for filing the actual claim. Look on the back of your insurance card, which should be in your car console or glove box, for the number to report an accident/claim.

Here's a summary of this fairly long section:

- Keep your driving record clean.
- Kiss Mom and Dad's ass and continue on their car insurance coverage for additional discounts (you can pay them monthly).
- Remember to get at least the minimum required insurance dictated by your state. See https://www.nerdwallet.com/blog/insurance/car-insurance.
- Before you buy a new or used car, get three quotes from insurance agents (your parents' insurer and two others) to use in your budget projections to see whether you can afford the monthly costs of the car and associated insurance premiums.
- With a used car, make sure you are covered (at a minimum) against liability and uninsured/underinsured motorists (and any other state-mandated coverage).
- With a new car and no loan, get full coverage to replace your albeit depreciating investment. Budget accordingly.
- A new car with a loan or a leased vehicle will require full coverage. Plan for this cost.
- Establish your cash reserve, raise your deductible and lower monthly premiums.
- Carry your proof of insurance in the car or on your person at all times.
- Turn twenty-five already and lower those premiums! What are you waiting for?

Now that we've got all things "car" out of the way, we can focus on your living arrangements.

Chapter 9

Where Do You Plan to Live?

A T THIS POINT in the book, it probably goes without saying that this is one of the key financial decisions you'll have to make when you graduate from high school. If it weren't a key financial decision, it wouldn't be in these pages, right? Right.

Some of you will be heading off to college and have your boarding established through university housing, while others will enter the workforce for the first time and figure out if you'll live at home or find a place of your own. Much of this decision rests on your relationship with your parents and/or their ability to continue to support you now that you've hit the magical age of eighteen. If you choose to pack up and leave your home behind, I want to make sure you're prepared for the financial (as well as the social) changes you'll encounter.

You've got several options once you drive away, leaving your parents waving or flipping you off in the rearview mirror (depending on your relationship).

- Stay with friends, which is cheap or free, depending on your relationship and length of stay. Chances are, the longer you stay without paying rent, the shorter your friendship will last.
- Rent a place by yourself, which is potentially expensive, depending on taste and location.
- Rent with a friend or group of friends to spread the costs. This could change the dynamic of your friendship or, conversely, be the best time of your life.
- Buy a condo, town home, house, or apartment, which is a big step for many and financially unrealistic for most just graduating high school.
- Lastly, you could choose to stay with your parents, which would allow you to save up for any of the previously described options.

The choice really depends on your goals, financial situation, and previous experiences with living arrangements. This could go as far back as rooming with brothers and sisters, to experiences on class trips or summer camps that exposed you to snoring roommates or friends cutting their toenails while you were trying to eat a piece of pizza. This section will expose you to the things that you may not have considered when you were sitting around the coffee shop dreaming about living in the big city or your rural hamlet postgraduation.

The place you choose to live needs to fit your budget and may need to be close to public transportation, depending on your car situation. Do you want to be close to work or friends, or close to amenities such as grocery stores or restaurants? There's a lot that goes into this decision. I've broken down each option to provide things to consider. Don't rush this decision. You'll regret being stuck in a yearlong lease paying $750 per month next to a neighbor who parties until four in the morning every single night of the week. Unless that's what you're looking for.

It may make more sense to think about where you want to end up. If your ultimate goal is to have your own house within five years, then you should plan accordingly.

If I ask you whether you can see yourself living with your parents for the next five years while saving for a down payment, would your eyes start to bleed or smoke shoot from your ears? This may be a sign that you need to move out immediately and find the cheapest rental property possible. You will ultimately need to temper your house-purchase expectations, because you've just added an additional monthly expense that used to be called "savings." If hemorrhagic bleeding and/or human combustion do not occur, then you could plan to save on rent, stay with your parents, and save enough for a down payment.

Living with Your Parents and Saving for a Down Payment

Set a goal and share that goal with your parents. If you plan to save enough for a down payment in five years (for instance), do these things:

- Review your budget.
- Use a mortgage calculator to determine the monthly payments.
  - ◦ Factor in property tax and homeowner's insurance
  - ◦ Make sure your budget will accommodate the monthly payments
- Set a savings goal to achieve the down payment by a certain date.
- Inform your parents on how long you plan to stay.
- Don't forget to sit down and figure out the ground rules for living in their house postgraduation.

- Ask whether they expect you to pay rent, since this will factor into available savings.
- Will there be a curfew, and if so, what time? Can you live we these expectations?
- Will you still be able to use the car? If so, what are the costs, if any, that you will be responsible for, such as insurance, gas, or routine maintenance?
- What kind of chores will you be expected to do while you live under their roof? Again, are these terms acceptable?

Take the initiative to get all this out in the open. As awkward as it may feel, it will benefit both sides in the long run.

If your ultimate goal is to purchase a home, set up time to go through the costs of home ownership with your parents. If there is a day of the month that Mom or Dad pays the bills, sit with him/her to understand monthly expenses. These won't be dollar for dollar the same as your future home costs, but there will be costs that you haven't thought of and I won't have listed here owing to regional differences, such as snow removal, lawn care, alarm services, and so on. This time will prove incredibly valuable when budgeting for your new home. Most new home buyers make the mistake of budgeting only for the down payment, overall purchase price and subsequent mortgage payment, but many other components will affect your budget. Here are several to consider when thinking about first-time home ownership:

- Homeowner's insurance (most times rolled into escrow payment within mortgage)
- Property taxes (most times rolled into escrow payment within mortgage)
- Association fees (if a condo or townhome)
- Utilities:
  - Gas (furnace, stove/oven, hot-water heater, dryer, etc.)
  - Electricity (lights, washer/dryer, baseboard heat [some houses], appliances, etc.)
  - Water (drinking, washing clothes and dishes, toilet/shower, etc.)
- Waste removal—trash pickup
- Home phone, if you choose to have one
- Internet service
- Cable or DISH television service (if you choose to have it)
- Security service such as ADT (if needed)
- Home-maintenance costs
  - Tools, you'll need tools (borrow these or look for organizations that loan tools)

- ❑ Plumbing supplies
- ❑ Paint
- ❑ Landscaping items (plants, soil, mulch… more expensive than you think)
- Furnishings (couch, bed, television, chairs, table, dishes, etc.)
- Parking costs, especially if apartment or city-permit parking
- Emergency plumbing services
- Furnace / air conditioner replacement (check during home inspection and plan accordingly). This may cost several thousand dollars. My furnace/central air replacement was recently estimated at $7,500.
- Roof replacement (check during home inspection and plan accordingly). Depending on square footage, this will cost several thousands of dollars. Ours was recently replaced due to wind damage. We paid the homeowner's insurance deductible and nothing else. Would have been $10,000 for a home with 1,440 square footage.

Here are chores that you'll by responsible for with a new home:

- Cutting the grass
- Watering the lawn
- Trimming shrubs
- Shoveling the sidewalk (northern states)
- Painting exterior/interior
- Plumbing, such as fixing leaky faucets and pipes, snaking out drains
- Cleaning out gutters in the fall
- Raking the leaves (autumn, non-desert states)
- General property maintenance, such as fixing a mailbox, patching chipped concrete, replacing shingles, and so on

Escrow. Sorry, I feel like I've thrown this term around but haven't clearly defined what this is. Escrow is an account where a portion of your monthly mortgage payment goes to pay your homeowner's insurance and your annual property tax obligations. This account is in your best interest, so you don't forget to pay these vital expenses. Think of it this way, if you have a mortgage payment of $1,100 per month, $250 of this may go towards the homeowner's insurance and property tax. The other $850 will go towards the principal and interest on the loan balance. Be prepared to see your mortgage balance hover and seemingly never decrease for the first couple of years because most of the payment is going towards interest on the loan. Rest assured, this is better than renting and flushing your monthly rent payment down the toilet, assuming you have the money to afford a house.

Coming Up with the Down Payment

The general rule of thumb when determining the down payment on your new home is 20 percent of the overall purchase price. That's $40,000 on a $200,000 home. Eeeeesh, that seems like a lot, doesn't it? It is, but that figure stems from avoiding what is called private mortgage insurance (PMI). PMI is an insurance you pay for the added risk you pose to your mortgage provider because of a lower down payment. The chance of a borrower defaulting on a mortgage is greater for someone who hasn't invested 20 percent of the home value. This additional monthly payment (PMI) varies per mortgage and is based on credit history and original down payment. PMI rates can range from 0.3 percent to 1.5 percent per year, and this fee is paid until the loan-to-asset ratio is roughly 80 percent (Bankrate.com, 2018). In other words, on a $200,000 loan, you would pay an additional $50 to $250 per month until you have 20 percent equity in your home. That's an additional $600 to $3,000 per year that doesn't go toward paying off your home loan and doesn't go toward equity in that home. As a point of clarification, the word "equity" is the dollar value you have invested in the home. For example, if your home is worth (assessed value) $200,000 and your remaining loan value is $150,000, you have $50,000 of equity in your home.

You are not required to have 20 percent down, and it may make sense to buy the house with less than 20 percent down, since you are an owner rather than a renter and building equity. You could offset the PMI with a renter of your own and build equity that much quicker by applying the rent to the mortgage payment to eliminate that extra expense (PMI) more quickly. Be aware that some loan types require a minimum of five years before you can rid yourself of PMI. This is the case with FHA loans.

Renting

If you have to move out owing to differences with your parents or just because you want to strike out on your own to experience life on your terms, take a second and think about this decision. Actually, take a few days to a week and truly explore why it is that you "have to" move out right now.

- What do you have saved up?
- Do have a job lined up?
- Can you move back home if it doesn't work out?
- Will you have to sign a lease that will force you to pay even if it doesn't work out?
- How much rent can you afford?

Experts differ on exactly how much of your take-home income should be spent on rent. A good rule of thumb is 25 percent of after-tax income. In our example, our take-home pay averages $1,647 per month, so $412 of that can go toward rent. You'll find that $412 won't go very far and that renting with friends may be your only solution. Generally, 15 percent of take-home pay is considered for paying off debt, so presumably, if you stay out of debt, you could add an additional 15 percent on top of the 25 percent allotment for rent. At 40 percent of take-home pay, you would be looking at $659 per month available for rent.

I am trying to impress upon you that this is an important decision and should be treated as such. Don't bite off more than you can chew. I remember how impulsive I was at your age; if I wanted something, I figured out a way to get it. But don't rush into a decision you'll regret.

Here are some of the costs you'll be exposed to as a renter:

- Monthly rent
- Groceries
- First and last month's rent up front
- Potentially a damage deposit in addition to first and last month's rent
- Furnishings (television, microwave, bed, etc.)
- Renter's insurance (a must)
- Utilities (gas, electric, water)
- Internet service
- Cable service (usually bundled with Internet)
- Parking fees (especially in a big city)
- Laundry services (unless you're close enough to use your parents' facilities)

If you can afford these costs, make sure you can afford them and more unless you feel like sitting in your awesome apartment eating bologna sandwiches every day because you can't afford to do anything else. Refer to the budget section to consider additional expenses that will impact cash flow.

My recommendation is to continue living with your parents for the foreseeable future and save those dollars toward a down payment on a house. You never know; along the way, you may decide that you want to go back to school, and the pot of money that you had been saving for a house could turn into tuition dollars, thus saving you (partially) from the student-debt conundrum that plagues this nation's youth. In conclusion, remember these tidbits:

- Try living at home with your parents to save up for a 20 percent down payment on a house.
- For a $150,000 home, save $30,000. This would be $500 per month (with no rate of return) over those five years.
- Establish ground rules with your parents for living under their roof postgraduation.
- If renting, budget 25 percent of take-home pay toward rent. If you are debt-free, you can extend that to a maximum of 40 percent. On our $1,647 monthly take home pay example, that's a rent range of $412 (25 percent) to $659 (40 percent) per month.
- Renting with friends will stretch your budget considerably, but make sure your friendship can endure the close spaces of a small apartment.
- Have fun for god sakes, this should be the best time of your life.

Chapter 10

Wrapping Up

I HOPE THIS WASN'T too time consuming or excruciatingly boring for you to read. Let's be clear, you are going to make mistakes in life; that is inevitable. And when it comes to finances, one person's mistake is another person's passion. By that, I mean not everyone wants to retire at age sixty or sixty-five (or whatever your number is). Your greatest pleasure in life may be to drive around in a tricked-out BMW or $60,000 Dodge pickup truck. If it brings you pleasure, then who am I to tell you that you shouldn't make that purchase? What I want you to glean from this book is that financial decisions have consequences, and the key is to know, before you make that purchase, what future milestones may be impacted. Knowing that and still taking on that ridiculous car payment or monstrous house payment, you'll have no regrets.

I've seen too many people look back in their forties, fifties, and sixties and regret that they didn't do things differently in their twenties and thirties. Don't always assume there will be more time or future pay raises that will allow you to catch up on retirement. For example, this is a classic: "I'll never retire. I'll work till I drop." That's one option, unless you can't. Retirement isn't always on your terms. Losing your job late in life or being forced to retire owing to health concerns happens. Don't let a similar reason catch you off guard, with the only thing standing between you and poverty being a shaky Social Security system. This shouldn't be something you need to worry about at your age, in the prime of your life, but unfortunately it is. If you don't worry about it, who will?

I'll leave you with one final statistic. A March 2016 Time.com report stated that 56 percent of Americans surveyed had less than $10,000 saved for retirement, with one out of three surveyed having saved nothing. That is appalling. They obviously didn't have this little gem given to them as a graduation gift. You don't have that excuse. Don't be these Americans. Get that health insurance, establish six months of living expenses as your cash reserve, enroll in disability insurance through your employer, and establish your retirement plan contributions up to the employer-matching percentage. This is a bare minimum. Next up is establishing and maximally funding a Roth IRA (if you qualify) and increasing your 401(k) contribution by a minimum of one percent per year, up to the annual maximum. If you do these things and still don't succeed, you can seek out my gravestone and burn this book on it. Just my grave, though; leave my wife's alone, please.

Oh, and enjoy the ride. You're only eighteen once—and nineteen, twenty, twenty-one...it's really a dumb saying, to be honest. Sorry.

PS You could have skipped the previous pages and just read this checklist (next page), and you would have been just as well off.

Chapter 11

Final Checklist

1. **Ask your parents whether you are still covered by their health insurance once you graduate. If not, visit HealthCare.gov or search for temporary health insurance options (typically three months) and get insurance.**
   - Consider selecting a higher deductible ($1,000 to $2,500) to reduce the monthly premium. Make sure your cash reserve is established to cover the deductible, if needed.
   - Read the fine print to ensure any pre-existing conditions are not excluded from this new policy.
   - Check on the ability to renew the policy (if this is a short-term policy) in case you don't secure employment with health benefits within three months of policy start date.
   - Shop around and talk with your parents about a suitable policy. Most important variables are: deductible, co-insurance options (shoot for 80/20), and maximum out of pocket for period (shoot for $1Million to cover catastrophic diagnosis).

2. **Do you have a savings account set up for your cash reserve?**
   - **Pay yourself first.** After your essentials are covered for the month, this should be the first expense you pay to your savings account.
     - Shoot for saving at least 15 percent of your take-home pay per month and more if you have it available (this will include your retirement savings plan at work).
     - If you don't have a savings account, set up time this week to walk into a local bank and establish an account or go online and pick an Internet banking institution to establish an account.
     - Make the savings systematic from your direct-deposited paycheck.

3. **Monitor your cash flow for the first two months to establish your budget.**
   - Keep a spreadsheet, and document where your paycheck is being spent.

4. **Identify your essential expenses (the ones you literally can't live without) and multiply those by six months. This is your cash-reserve goal amount.**
   - Save it and maintain it.

5. **Do you have a job lined up?**
   - Establish your benefits.
     - Health insurance should be priority #1. Consider an HSA if you're healthy and your employer matches contributions.
     - Establish disability insurance for the maximum allowed, preferably with after-tax premiums.
     - Begin retirement contributions up to the employer matching percentage (increase the contribution by 1 percent at least annually).

6. **Where will you live?**
   - If you are staying with parents, have that talk and set/get expectations for your continued stay, so everyone is on the same page.
   - Make sure to ask whether your parents are still planning to claim you as a dependent on their taxes, as that will affect how you file your tax return.
   - If renting, budget up to 25 percent of take-home pay (up to 40 percent if debt-free) towards this monthly cost.
   - If renting with roommates, sit down and assess your budget and do the exercises that we talked about earlier. Can you afford this place? Does it meet your location requirements for work and amenities? Truly consider whether you can live with your roommates long term and make sure your decision wasn't made in a drunken euphoria.
   - Are you planning to buy a house, condo, townhouse or apartment?
     - Have you reviewed the list of anticipated expenses and responsibilities that come with a new home?
     - How much house can you afford? Remember to include property tax, insurance and potentially PMI in your cost estimates.
       - Budget up to 40 percent of monthly take-home pay if debt-free (25 percent with debt).
     - What is your timeframe? Determine how much you need to save.
     - Can you save for a 20 percent down payment to avoid PMI payments? This is the ideal scenario but can definitely make sense even if you don't have the full 20 percent.
     - Consider roommates to help cover your mortgage payments.

7. **What will you drive?**
   - If you're driving the car your parents gave you, continue driving this into the ground, and save what would have been your monthly payment. This will allow you to buy a car with cash in the future

(buy something that's at least two to three years old, and try to get a warranty if at all possible).

- If you're planning on leasing, consider these points:
  - Can you restrict your mileage to the guideline restrictions of ten, twelve, or fifteen thousand miles?
  - Are you planning to pay at least $250 per month and $2,000 every three years as an up-front cost to lease the vehicle? You may end up doing this the rest of your life. Is that what you want?
  - Remember that you don't own this car and must abide by the terms of the lease.
  - Can you afford full coverage car insurance? Get a quote before you sign the paperwork.
- If you are buying new, consider these points:
  - Is your cash reserve established?
  - Can you afford a down payment? Do the math. Does this work in your budget?
  - Can you afford the monthly payment? Again, does this fit into your budget?
  - Are you planning to drive this car for the next ten to fifteen years? You should.
  - How much will this limit your cash flow to do other things with your friends?
  - How much is the insurance? Can you afford full coverage? Get three quotes before you sign the new car paperwork.
  - Don't buy the extended warranty or rust protection.
  - Don't buy any add-ons from the dealership.
- If you are buying used, consider these points:
  - Find out what the markup is. Go to the Kelly Blue Book website (KBB.com) and look up the value of this car with the amenities offered. Make sure you're not getting screwed.
  - A two- to three-year-old car is typically the best value.
  - Try to get a warranty (typically offered by dealerships), but know the terms of that warranty.
  - If you are not buying from a respectable dealership, have the car inspected by a mechanic prior to buying.

8. **Get car insurance.**
   - Stay on your parents' insurance if at all possible; this will be cheaper.
   - If you have an older used car, at a minimum, get liability coverage (personal injury and property) and uninsured/underinsured motorist protection.
   - If you have a new car with a loan or a lease, you will be obligated to insure with full coverage. This will be expensive.

9. **Get some sort of disability insurance once you're employed.**
   - Preferably get this through your employer up to the maximum offered (STD and LTD).
   - If it's offered, select the after-tax premium option so the benefits are paid tax-free.

10. **To expand on the 401(k) or 403(b) retirement accounts. Establish your workplace retirement account immediately, especially if your employer matches contributions.**
    - Contribute up to the employer-matching percentage. If they offer a 3 percent match if you contribute 3 percent, then do it. If they require 6 percent to match 4.5 percent, contribute the full 6 percent.
      - Increase your percentage by 1 percent each year up to the maximum allowed.
    - Select the Roth 401(k) option (if available).
    - Choose a target fund for your presumed age of retirement (if available). You can change the allocation percentages once you determine your tolerance for risk.

11. **File your tax return by the business day closest to April 15.**
    - Ask your parents whether they are claiming you as a dependent.
    - File Form 1040EZ if you can.
    - Use the Free File software option on IRS.gov (IRS.gov/freefile).

12. **LAST BUT NOT LEAST, HAVE FUN WHILE BEING A GOOD PERSON! NOBODY LIKES A JERK, WHETHER YOUR RICH OR POOR.**

www.ingramcontent.com/pod-product-compliance
Lightning Source LLC
Chambersburg PA
CBHW070108210526
45170CB00013B/793